People and Places

A Memoir

Best wishes
Jacomena Maybeck
1993

Jacomena Maybeck

Stonegarden Press
Berkeley, 1992

ISBN: 1-879042-01-0
Printed in the United States of America

Design by
Andrea DuFlon

Composition by
Terri Castell-Catanesi

Printing by
McNaughton & Gunn

Published by
Stonegarden Press
2851 Buena Vista
Berkeley, CA 94708

All photos, except those noted, are taken from Jacomena Maybeck's family album. Cover photo by Gui de Angulo. Cover motif by Jacomena Maybeck.

Jacomena Maybeck. (Photo Gui de Angulo)

One

Holland

"Tell me about yourself. Where did you come from?" What a great question! In this family it's mostly asked of a Maybeck, as though I had been found in a cabbage! But I love to look back to my parents and let the beautiful Dutch names flow over my tongue. My father, Piet Jan Rensius van Huizen. My mother, Helene Kleyn-Schoorel—she was always called Lane. My mother's mother, Oma (grandmother) Adriana de Graf, my mother's sisters, Tante (aunt) Marie and Tante Anna, her sister-in-law, Tante Maal, and her brother, Oom (uncle) Nick. They were loving background and companions when my father went away on a sugar campaign to Portugal, or Africa, or Cuba. My father was a sugar chemist. He always called a job a campaign.

1

My father was the eldest of seven children of another family in North Holland. They lived and worked in the family grocery store, Sylstraat 6, Haarlem. When I visited Holland after the war in 1946 I saw that sign hanging over the door. I believe the store was sold and the sign came down about 1988.

My father had asthma and told us he often went out and walked the dikes to get some air and peace. When he was young, life must have been hard for him. He went to the University of Delft and studied chemistry under the famous van Hoff. At nineteen he was offered a job in a sugar refinery in Surabaya, Java. He went there and left his big family, and the girl he most liked, Helene Kleyn-Schoorel. She lived with her father and mother in Logdrecht, a village near a dike. Their house was built right against the dike, and in rainstorms the basement flooded. This basement was the stables for the family horses as well as the wine cellar. The horses were led away to high ground, but the wine bottles floated about and clanked against the walls. Dr. Kleyn-Schoorel often had to go out at night—stormy or not—to see a sick patient, and he went in his horse carriage. It was a hard life, and he became an alcoholic and ran away with his nurse. Grandmother got a divorce—a terrible scandal! This must have been in 1850.

Anyway, my father, young Piet van Huizen, went

to Java and the sugar mill. He saved his money and in two or three years he was able to return to Holland and the girl he liked so much, Helene. They were married and honeymooned through Switzerland and across the Mediterranean, the Red Sea, Ceylon, British India and so to Java, the Dutch Colony. They were a pretty dashing couple, from the photos.

They were given a concrete house with one side open, like all the houses, seven servants, free sugar, and free medical care. They learned to wear the sarong and white linen jacket. And now the tall, blue-eyed, curly-haired Dutch girl, my mother, who loved cold weather, had to adapt to heat and a strange language, too. Fortunately she had a sense of adventure, and also fortunately her sister was there—she had married a doctor and come out to the Colony earlier. I was born in Surabaya in 1901. They said the doctor was drunk and he had to be found and brought back to do his job. Anyway, there I was, a bald-headed girl child, named for my two grandmothers, Jacomena and Adriana.

My father had saved his money, as usual, and he planned to go back to Holland and to the university. When I was seven months old they took that long journey back.

I don't know where we lived, but I remember one day several aunts came over and a man with a black bag went upstairs to my mother. My father and the aunts waited and at last he came down. "It's a boy," he said. So I had a brother, Pieter. I was two.

Time went on and my father's money ran out as usual. No jobs in Holland for sugar chemists! So he took a job in a sugar plantation in Portugal. He learned Portuguese; he always learned the language of his work country. And he did love to travel.

My mother, Pieter, and I now went to live with Oma Kleyn-Schoorel, my mother's mother, and about then we began to make the lovely visits to Haarlem and the other grandmother. I remember when the maid scrubbed the tiled hallways I was allowed to wear wooden shoes like hers and slosh around too. And the store in Haarlem became familiar to me. We went there weekends and slept in the wall beds. They had doors to close in daytime, also a hook in the ceiling to hang a baby bed and a shelf on the wall for a clock and a book. A maid came up at seven or eight and brought the tea and brown bread, cheese and dried figs.

I see now what a wonderful family it was! First came Opa (grandfather) Piet van Huizen, Sr., head of the family. He had been a lithographer on stone, but he was thought a bit frail, and got special care. Oma, my van Huizen grandmother, was tall and vigorous, full of energy and spirit, with blue eyes and curly hair. All the brown eyes in my family came from Opa, right through to my father and my twin daughters.

At eighty-four Oma was still riding her bicycle all over Haarlem to visit her friends. The family all stayed together, all the children, until she died. Then they all got married and had their own homes. Most of them were fifty by then.

There was Karel, often in the office when we visited, and Aunt Mien of the red hair was next, then Tante Anna, playful and loving—I adored her! Tante Rie was musical and fashionable and married an organist later. Tante Agnes was domestic, and Oom Jo became a naval officer. They all came and went about the store and gathered in the long dining room for big noisy meals. In the afternoon Oma tended her garden behind the living room while I sat on the floor surrounded by wonderful little boxes and pencils and pads and strings and clips. I still love paper and pens.

They had a garden behind the shop, and then a staircase going up the stairs which was lined with blue and white Dutch tiles—a fortune in tiles, but they didn't know it! And you'd go up there and there were all the bedrooms for everybody. Next to that there was a warehouse where they measured flour and candled eggs! I remember those things! It was a great place to visit.

And then my uncle, my mother's brother, Nick

Kleyn-Schoorel, went to California! I think he must have read about it in a magazine. No one else in our family had ever gone anywhere, except the Indies, you know. Anyway, Uncle Nick came to California and he found a little gold mine up on Mount Shasta. He kept writing to his sister and my father that they should come out and enjoy it with him. My father apparently was always ready to go somewhere, and this time my mother said, "Piet, I'm not going to stay behind. I'm going with you." And so they packed up and they went to California

I member, *vaguely*—I was seven years old—being at the wharf. We went on the steamship *Valandam*. It must have been 1908, and all the family, uncles and aunts and nephews and nieces all came to the wharf to see us off, to see the ship sail. We never saw them again.

*Lane van Huizen, Piet, and Jacomena,
just before leaving for California.*

Two

Crockett, Uncle Nick,
The Maybecks

We got to New York, and it was snowing, and we had to go through customs, and those warehouses. It was very cold. But we got on a train and we came to California through the South. We must have come through Georgia and up above New Orleans, and then Texas, and we saw the Indian women sitting in the station, selling beads. We got to Los Angeles, and my mother wrote back to her sisters, "This is the most beautiful place I've ever seen!" There were orange trees in bloom and packs of geraniums in full bloom...Of course Los Angeles in 1908 was a small town! Then we came to Oakland and they had just had that bad earthquake in San Francisco, and there was a lot of devastation. But

9

we didn't go there; my uncle was building a little house in Fruitvale. His little vein of gold had run out so he borrowed my father's money and they built that house, while we lived in it, and then they sold it and they built another one in Mill Valley. But by this time my father's funds were running very low, and he decided he had better go back to chemistry. So he got a job in Crockett as Chief Chemist of the California-Hawaiian Sugar Refinery. It was a very big place and he had the laboratory that was plastered to the south side of the building.

We lived in Crockett then, on the hill. I went to school there, to the fifth grade...is that possible? There must have been something in between. Another house, probably. More money gone.

Crockett was a company town, and there were many, many Portuguese people who lived along the railroad. They lived very tumultuous lives, and their children had bugs in their hair. They went to school and you'd sit behind one, and it was very interesting to watch! The Portuguese also had fights; we went to the funeral of a little girl who was killed because her parents fought together and a gun went off! The main street of Crockett was only about five blocks long; it was lined on both sides by saloons, and you *never walked down* that street after five o'clock because it was full of Portuguese trying to get a high on.

My mother was always my very good companion, and I began to find out what she enjoyed doing. She had brought beautiful clothes with her from Holland, with leg-of-mutton sleeves and high collars, in satins, but she couldn't really wear them very often in Crockett. So she found a seamstress who could make things for her, and I went along with my mother when the seamstress measured her. I thought this was very important. She made my mother a suit of tan-colored gabardine, with a long skirt and a jacket, and this was her American outfit.

My mother was tall and slim. I look like her, I think, except she had curly hair, which I always envied. She had a lovely smile and she was always very gracious to people.

My father was quite dashing. He had a mustache and brown hair, and sparkly brown eyes. I just took him for granted, I guess; I thought he was a nice person to have around and that was about it. I didn't notice his clothes until afterwards, after we bought the ranch in Ukiah and he began to wear knickers and heavy outdoor hose and boots and sunhats.

Then my uncle Nick pops into the picture again.

By this time he had married the daughter of a professor at U.C., Professor Isaak Flagg. My aunt Amy was a Gibson Girl; she was very pretty, and she was very frivolous, and she *only* went to college so that she could go to the college dances. My uncle Nick was gay and debonair, and he had a horse and buggy, and I don't know what they lived on. They certainly lived with Grandpa Flagg for a while. I think they borrowed money from him.

Grandpa Flagg had a place in Ukiah, three miles out on Low Gap road, west of Ukiah. There was a creek on that property and on this creek Bernard Maybeck, the architect, had built his friend Professor Flagg a country house, a lodge, with a great big stone fireplace and upstairs a little sleeping loft and a big porch. Grandpa Flagg used to go there for summers.

Well, Amy, who married my Uncle Nick, would go out there too, and so when they were married, she and Nick both naturally went out and stayed in the lodge for vacations. Uncle Nick, who was an explorer, was very curious about the rest of that country: what was behind that road to Low Gap, where did that creek came from....So he hiked up into the hills, following little country roads, and he found little homes, four or five places—we used to call them "the places"—where people lived on homesteaded land. He talked several of these people into selling

Uncle Nick.

him a part of their homesteaded acre, or selling him
the whole thing, and he built several small, very
attractive houses on some of those places. This was
entirely his own idea.

But he and Amy lived in that Maybeck lodge
quite a bit. We came up for the summers, through
them, because Nick was my mother's brother. My
father and mother and Pieter and I began to go up
there and camp on our vacations. The Maybecks
were camping up there when we were camping up
there. The lodge was not big enough for all of us, so
if Mr. and Mrs. Maybeck came they would stay in
the lodge and the rest of us just all camped outside,
wherever. That's how we got to know each other.
The Maybecks were there from the very beginning
of our life there; we saw them all summer. I knew
Wallen, the Maybeck's son, from the time he was
thirteen and I was ten.

Then began the friendship between Kerna, the
Maybeck's daughter, and me. I met Kerna on this
camping activity, when we would go up to the lodge
on the creek and all go swimming. We didn't have
bathing suits; we simply swam in overalls, or anything we had. Of course we kids loved it up there,
Wallen, aged thirteen, and I, ten, Kerna, nine, and
my brother Pieter, nine too.

Kerna was the only one who was interesting to

me, because I could play with her. Although Wallen was kindly and friendly toward us, he didn't pay any attention to us because he wanted to go off hiking with my father and Maybeck and Uncle Nick. They went up hunting for various things, up on the ridge. My uncle showed Maybeck that steep, steep trail up to the ridge, and the country up there, and Maybeck bought two thousand acres of it to camp on. But he hardly ever used it, and he sold it a few years later.

Maybeck never had a lot of money. He got big assignments and then there were big payments, and they lived on those, and then maybe would come another assignment. It was very much a hand-to-mouth kind of living. The land was there; when they didn't get an assignment to build a house, Mrs. Maybeck saw to it that they had money by borrowing on the land or selling some.

They bought this land up here in North Berkeley all in one piece. Three men did it together, and they bought from Cedar Street up to Rose Street, a long strip, which was called La Loma Park. They each took a third of it. I think Maybeck had ten or twelve acres. That was this part, where my house is. The land probably cost fifty dollars an acre. I have a map that is labeled 1908—it's not a deed, just a map of this area. Maybe Maybeck bought it in 1915. He must have had some money around 1915 from building the Palace of Fine Arts at the Fair.

When I first saw them up at Ukiah, Maybeck and Mrs. Maybeck were that mysterious middle age that older people always were. You had no idea really how old older people were; they were just older. Since they were vigorous, and walking and talking and taking trips and building important buildings, they couldn't have been so very old. Ben must have been in his early fifties or late forties. He was not a physical type. My uncle was a dashing, moving, physical type, my father also; they later called him the Flying Dutchman. But Mr. Maybeck kept his feet on the ground; he moved around everywhere, he went everywhere, but always with great dignity. He was very kind; he was sociable. He was interested in people; he was gentle.

His looks…that's another thing kids aren't interested in, the looks of older people. They like them the way they are, but they don't concentrate on how they look. We were aware that Maybeck had a white beard, and that made him Santa Claus. We were aware of the fact that my father and my uncle shaved; they had clean-cut faces. We were aware that Mrs. Maybeck had a lot of funny clothes; she always wore a lot of clothes. Mostly she made them herself. I was aware that my mother was very particular about clothes, and if she could she had them made for her, because she was used to that in Holland. Now, Mrs. Maybeck, I learned later, got a lot of her clothes from the second hand stores and the Mobilized Women, because the Maybecks were going through a poor streak, and she didn't like to shop. Besides, she loved to change and dye and adjust clothes like that to her own needs, which were different from everybody else's.

Mrs. Maybeck was small, and lively looking, with curly grey hair, and big grey eyes; she had a sharp voice, and was given to shouts of laughter if something struck her funny. She loved to wear lacy sleeves and silks and bits of satin and velvet. She sometimes made one-piece dresses out of yards of corduroy, so that she could just slip them on and she was dressed. A very good idea; it's what the housecoat is today.

She didn't go on hikes. The hikes were taken by my father, Maybeck, Uncle Nick and Wallen. They were the hikers. They hiked up the ridge. Kerna and I wanted to go too, but we weren't invited, and so we sat and cut paper dolls out of the magazines.

Wallen was the "man" of the group of children, and he was very nice looking, and he was very nice mannered, and naturally I thought he was wonderful. But I could play with paper dolls with Kerna, and I couldn't play with Wallen. But I could look at him, and admire him. And I did.

For many years we all rode and hiked and sang together in the sunsets. I sat beside Wallen in a shy glow of love and admiration, and deep inside I knew I would some day marry him.

Three

Pine Ridge, High School

So my parents got to know the Ukiah country, and they fell in love with it. My father had asthma, and he wanted to get out of the laboratory. So in 1913 he bought a hundred acres of land from Uncle Nick, up on Pine Ridge road. We planned to build on it.

We were still living in Crockett, but somehow my parents were deciding to go up and build in that wild country. I don't know how they planned to make a living there. But anyway, in the summer of 1913 my father rented a house in the town of Ukiah and left my mother and my brother and me there, and went to Cuba on a campaign in a sugar factory. That was money for the ranch. (War came in 1914 and Dad nearly didn't get back; he wasn't a citizen yet.)

Then in 1916 we moved to Uncle Nick's ranch, into a charming little house he had built on "spec." Big windows and a big fireplace—the view was splendid. We also had a barn. I don't know why, we only had a pet pig, but somehow we acquired a big white horse, too.

Now we had to make a dirt road to our hundred acres and build a house. What courage my parents had, Lane and Piet van Huizen! My father read a book. He always read a book before starting a great adventure. I think it was called *Little Landers,* by Albert Hubbard. First a level path to a large flat knoll, not too far from a never-dry spring. No one could live up in that country without a good spring for water. Then we made the path into a road, ourselves. We decided on a homesite, on the north edge of the flat, leaving the south and east ends for mother's garden.

Next we made a path up the hill to a little forest of pines and began to cut trees for the house walls, four- to six-inch straight and strong pines. Pieter and I trimmed and peeled them and all four of us carried them down the hill. Too steep for the horse. Enough poles to make the framework for the house. Enough poles to make roof beams and rafters. Then somehow boards for sheathing and shingles were brought in. Did our horse do that?

We built a living room, kitchen—wood stove—

and bedrooms, one for Dad and Mother, one for Pieter and me (though he soon had his own cabin). Big windows that slid open. Little entry porch. A little basement for shelves of canned fruit from the trees Dad soon planted—after his acre of watermelons, which no one knew what to do with.

We hung up mother's rugs and pictures. We made a big couch over an army cot. We got Mother's piano in. We got shelves for our books and a telephone—party line—one long, two short.

Pieter and I kept growing and soon had a horse each, and we still had the old white horse. She had drawn Tante Anna to our place on a sled with a chair on it, over our tiny road! Tante Anna had been visiting a daughter in Java and was going home to Holland.

My mother had begun to wear clothes she could hike in, because they had often hiked up to our little piece of land from the Flagg lodge. Then later, she felt she should ride horseback because I was riding horseback, and we made divided riding skirts for ourselves, because nobody wore blue jeans then. Women didn't wear pants in those days.

When I finished grammar school I had to go to high school. I had to live in town, somehow or other. The first year I stayed with my Uncle Nick, and walked those three miles to high school. On those walks my cousin Nicki and I walked together. I had

21

The House on Low Gap Road.

The Old White horse.

met the Benson family; Dr. Benson was an Episcopal minister; there were seven children in that family. So soon Nicki and I journeyed down those three miles with the Benson girls, who came up the hill to meet us—and the Benson boys, of course. Walking down the three miles we passed a vineyard, and that was the place where they arrived from their place on the way to school. We joined forces there and we all went on together. That was very pleasant.

I met the Benson family through my uncle. I don't know how they got to know my uncle, but they did, and they would come up to his place. Uncle Nick was very sociable; he began to know everybody. He was tall and good looking and had very charming manners. He could tell little stories and jokes, and he could talk people into anything. He talked Grandpa Flagg into lending him money and letting him marry his daughter. He came from Holland as rather a rascal who didn't want to go to medical school. They had shipped him out. He immediately got a horse and buggy and a guitar, so he could sing songs, and take people for rides in the buggy. He was a charmer.

Since there were seven children in the Benson family, of course there was one to fit any need. I made friends with Mary, the oldest daughter, and Huntington, the oldest son, and presently I was going to their house on weekends after school.

My second year in high school I lived with my mother's friend who had a daughter my age, and we went to high school together. They had a house that was attached to a tannery, on that same road.

The next year I lived with my mother's other friend. They were Welsh, and they had a son named Ewan. Ewan would sit at the dining table and eat buttered bread with syrup on it; that seemed to be a national dish. I'd never seen it eaten before. He loved that. It was called "dusdus." Syrup was called treacle.

Well, the next year my mother put me with *another* friend of hers in town, an old lady who had an enormous Victorian house and an acre of garden around it, trees and garden. She had a gardener to take care of it. She had a little black spaniel. I slept on the third floor and she and the spaniel slept on the second floor. She sent him up to wake me in the morning, and he'd come running up the stairs and jump on my bed and want to play. So I would get up and play, and we'd go down and have breakfast, and I'd walk to school from there.

There was just one black girl in that high school of two hundred kids, and I used to walk along with her sometimes. One day I was walking along and she tumbled into a ditch next to the path. I went for help. I don't know what was the matter with her—

nobody did. I don't know what became of her then.

My brother was of course the joy of the family; he had been a beautiful little boy with curly blond hair and blue eyes, while I was a tall string of a girl with long hair. I always envied him. We were sort of...not enemies exactly, but we certainly were not very friendly. We competed for everything. And then presently he grew up; I noticed one day that he was as tall as my father, and I *immediately* changed my mind about him, and decided that he could be useful to me! He was attractive; he could take me to parties. That went on for quite a while; we became very good friends, very good companions. We were in our teens then. I was going to the Bensons' for weekends and Peter began to come, too. Now that he went to school he was Peter, not Pieter.

My brother had his own cut-down Ford, which was much admired in high school because it was painted blue and it had a leather strap over the hood, and you sat, if you were a passenger, on a rubber tire. (*He* must have had a seat!) Anyway pretty high school teachers all wanted to ride in my brother's convertible, such as it was; you were *right* down practically on the highway.

Later the Bensons came from their place to high school in a little Dodge convertible called Drucilla. Drucilla would hold about seven or eight of us if we piled up a little bit. I often went back home with them, and spent the weekend with them, and then I didn't have to try to get home. Getting home was a big problem. I had to walk ten miles, or somebody had to come with a horse and buggy to get me. When I was staying with that old lady I liked to go home, but I loved going to the Bensons', because there were nine of us at dinner, and Dr. Benson—he was a wonderful person—would read to us while we had our salads, and then the hot dinner would come. He read English novels; I've never seen them around since. I've never heard of anybody who read them, but we were fascinated. We read a little Dickens too. Then the girls would wash the dishes, and the boys went out in the half-dark and milked the cows. Pails of foamy milk came in. When the chores were done, we all came in, put on a record, and danced. Wonderful!

At bed time the girls went upstairs and the boys slept in the little rooms attached to the house in a long row. We called them the chicken house, but they were built as bedrooms for the five boys.

The Bensons began my intellectual life. It was the way they talked and the kind of things they talked about. Mr. Benson asked us what we read and thought. The children were all planning to go to college. Two boys became doctors. They all grew up and became distinguished.

Dr. Benson made me realize I had a mind and

must use it, so I began to want to go to college too. The Benson grandfather was president of Pomona College, in Claremont, and he had promised his grandchildren scholarships, after he dedicated a building to the college. He didn't know that there would be seven grandchildren!

So after I finished high school I took the county examinations and got a teacher's credential. I stayed up there another two years after I finished high school, because I had no money. I got a job in this little grammar school, with ten children, up on Pine Ridge. They gave me that school because the neighbors all knew me and my family. I taught school and saved my money for two years.

Some of the students were teenage boys, three or four of them, from the ranches, and *they* were a handful! But they also knew that I was well-known to their parents, and they had to mind me. They were always a little bit out of hand. It was like driving a team of very spirited horses. I was just twenty!

Then there were four little Indian children; the family lived in one of the cottages along the road, and these children were in the first and second grade. They knew almost no English. They sat and smiled and nodded their heads, and I would talk to them and let them draw pictures, and give them books to read, but they didn't know what they were reading. And I didn't know how to start teaching a whole new language to people who could barely speak their *own* language. They were just little kids! So really I was just baby-sitting them, that's really what I was doing.

Because I had so many children I would spend fifteen minutes on each class and then move on to the next class. I would give them things to do, reading, writing, drawing, and then I'd come back to them later.

It was very challenging. And I always had my little dog named Dinky who came with me and sat under my desk. Once or twice a year somebody from town would come and inspect us. When the inspector would come by this was always rather terrifying because I didn't know if I was doing the right thing. I was so untrained! I was just doing the very best I knew how! I was really very worried about those inspectors, but they were always very kind and felt that we were keeping the place in order, and the children must be learning *something.* One room, and a wood stove. And why did they stay there with me? Why didn't those children just take off into the woods? You know, you wonder. Of course, it was their parents. It would have come back to the parents, any infringements.

So I applied to Pomona, and was admitted. We were all going, and I would be going, too. Until I began to realize how far away Pomona was—near Los Angeles—and how expensive, and that Wallen was in Berkeley. I loved the idea of going to Pomona with Huntington and Geo and Dirk, but I loved Wallen, too. It was a great decision, and there was pain in it. So the boys left for the south and Mary and I went by train to Berkeley. It was a great turning point, and now I was headed for a new life.

Jacomena in college.

Four

College, Marriage

To me that train was a magic way of getting out of Ukiah valley and into the big world. Down to the Bay Area, across the bay to Berkeley, and to the little St. Margaret's House, and our rooms there. *There* I met Flo Jury—black bob and green eyes—and Flo Baker. They were my age. Mary Benson was doing graduate work so she was a serious student. We were just freshmen, and all eyes and ears and emotions.

U.C. Berkeley in 1923 was a rather small college in a quiet intellectual town. Ladies wore skirts, gloves, and hats to shop on Shattuck Avenue. Soon we all settled down in a sort of groove. In early morning we went to chapel; then we had our breakfast, and we all traipsed off to school and went to our classes. Flo Jury and I were in a number of classes together as freshmen, and we used to tramp across the campus *very* fast! I think of it now, how fast and determinedly we walked from one class to another. But you often only had ten minutes to make it! I majored in education, for the simple reason that I had to real choice: I had to figure out how I could earn a living when I graduated, so I thought, I'll prepare to be a teacher. (Of course what I *wanted* to do was take art. I took as much as I could.) They were very boring, those education courses, very boring. But nevertheless I got through, and I got a secondary teacher's credential, as well as a Bachelor of Arts degree.

Flo and I stayed together during that whole time. It seems to me that she left at one time to take some special training in law in Oregon, and then she came back again. We lived together at first in St. Margaret's House, and then a tiny woman named Madaleine, who was very intellectual and admired Flo, invited Flo into her sorority. Then Flo brought me along, because we had gotten to be very good friends. Yes, I was in a sorority! It was not exactly a sorority; at that time it was not a Greek letter sorority, it was a house for college women to live in, established by Mrs. Phoebe Hearst. She had given furniture and pictures to it.

So the first semester was in St. Margaret's House, and the second semester was in this in-between house. Then that group bought a house on Panoramic Way, and that's where I first went in as a real sorority girl. We wore gold pins, you know, pinned half way down on our sweaters. We wore these baggy sweaters, and down here somewhere, where your heart was supposed to be, we had our pin.

We had a good time in that house! It was a big old redwood house, and it had a porch. We could sit on the porch and watch the football crowds go up to the stadium. We went ourselves, very early, because we were following the teams, and took our lunches along. And we had college dates, of course. We invited professors to dine at the house with us, so we met some of the faculty. You could do that; a house could invite faculty members if they liked or admired them, and they'd come and have dinner with us. A lot of good talk. I sat next to Professor Lewis, of the Physics Department I think; he had on a starched shirt, or at least a portion of his shirt sort of bounced around; it kept popping out of his vest and being pushed back in again, like a piece of stiff cardboard. And we had parties that we invited boys to. I invited Wallen. We invited all kinds of boys to our dances.

So that was a good experience. I also could save a little money by being the housekeeper for the house. I planned the meals for the sorority; I planned the meals and did the shopping. The shopping was interesting to me because I would go to the stores and they would give us a discount, as a house, and then they would bring up these quantities, you know, twenty pounds or fifty pounds of flour, or twenty pounds of sugar; we'd buy in large quantities. That took planning and bargaining.

We had a Chinese cook, a very emotional Chinese cook, who smoked opium in his little lair behind the kitchen—because we could smell it! But since we didn't ever see him, we didn't feel we could chase him away. Once we decided we would tidy up the whole house, make it beautiful, so we swept and we washed, and we took lye and soap and washed the kitchen floor and bleached it down to natural wood. The Chinese cook came home and absolutely had a fit! Because he loved it painted, and he had painted it grey, and he immediately painted it grey again! So that was it.

I always went up to the ranch for the vacation. Flo came up there once, and Wallen and Kerna once rode their horses up from Berkeley. It took four days. Then my third year, after vacation, I got a job on Forest Avenue, down College Avenue, where I could get my board and room free for doing the cooking. It was a big house belonging to a professor and his wife who were in Europe. There were three women living in it. Nancy Up was one of them; she was one of the deans of women. There were two others; one of them stayed friends with me for a long time.

I lived there; I had a nice room. I would get home at five o'clock from school and I would dash in and cook whatever they had said they wanted me to cook. I had perfect faith in myself that I could do this. I learned to make fancy little salads with preserved pears and currants and Neufchatel cheese. I had learned to cook at the ranch; my mother and I just figured out what we wanted to eat and we helped each other. I learned to cook very fast and very simple meals up there.

For recreation there were always dances for the classes, freshman dances, sophomore dances…We joined the Cosmopolitan Club, which was full of foreign students, and this was interesting to us, to make friends with them a little, anyway, to observe them. And then there were dances at the St. Mark's Club, at the St. Mark's Church. Flo had fallen in love with a beautiful young man who was in the choir. Of course I had Wallen and took him down there, and other boys and girls gathered, and we made very good friends there. I still have Wendy, in San Francisco, who was a part of that. They had

Sunday night supper and Sunday night dances, and Sunday night parties. There was a lot of activity for young people at the St. Mark's Club.

We went walking up in the hills. We took picnics up in the hills. Of course we went to the football games, or any other kind of games that came along. They had parades in the football season, and they had the Pajamareno rally, whatever that was! They had big bonfires in the Greek Theater, and people went and sang and sat around.

And then occasionally you studied.

I wasn't seeing the Maybecks as much as I did later. I dated Wallen a lot, but I didn't come up to the Maybecks'. Kerna had gone away for a while—I guess she went to New York to work in a dental office. Anyway, she belonged to a very big house, Alpha Delta Phi, and she had her own much more sophisticated circle of friends than I had.

Occasionally the Ukiah people would come down and we'd see them, the Bensons. Then always summer vacations up on the ranch! I would get so lonesome for the ranch in June. The fog would come in, and I *hated* fog! I'd begin to long for the blue sky of the ranch. Although when I went back there I'd give up the college life for the whole summer, nevertheless it was lovely up there and I enjoyed it. I enjoyed my mother very much...and a few neighbor people.

36

But mostly we canned fruit, we gardened, we read a lot, and once a week we went to town, and that was a big business. I think we had a little Dodge, a one-seater, by then, and we bobbled down to town. We'd buy large quantities of groceries at one time. If we went down once a week we were lucky. But we had *all* our vegetables, *all* our water, and *all* our wood right out of that ranch. We all enjoyed it, my mother and I, and my brother who was there a lot of the time. My father was usually out in one of the sugar mills making his money for the rest of the year.

Wallen had gotten his first job at the telephone company the year I came to college, in '23. He graduated in '22 and went to work. So he went over to his job in the telephone building every morning with his father; they crossed the bay on the ferry boat. He liked that; you know, you could get grapefruit and prunes and wonderful coffee and get your shoes polished and it was such a nice way to go ... read your paper.

The first place the Maybecks had on the hill was a very big house. It had thirteen rooms and the entrance was down on the corner of La Loma and Buena Vista. There was an entrance path and there was a tree trunk that was totally covered with a mattress vine. The kids used to climb up there and bounce up and down. That was a strange thing, that mattress vine! Then you walked up this little trail, or path. I don't know whether there were stepping stones or whatever.

Mrs. Maybeck had a maid. Not in the country; they were only in the country for a week or so at a time. But whenever she lived in town she always had a maid. They had a big house and Mrs. Maybeck was used to being helped. This must have come from the east; after all, she came from New England, where Irish maids were the ordinary. She kept that tradition going here. I don't know where she got them.

When Wallen was a boy he went to private school at the corner of Derby and Bellrose Avenue. There's a corner there where there are a lot of low wooden buildings and a hedge, and that was a private school. Wallen went there because Maybeck had built the school. Wallen would start down from the hill across the fields, and he went a lot of the way on roller skates. He was the only boy in the school so he sat all by himself in a seat in the back. He never complained, but I'm sure he didn't like it. But he had a lot of trouble that way; they kept trying to make him into Little Lord Fauntleroy. They wanted his hair long and curly, and they made him wear velvet suits! He finally rebelled and just began to wear corduroy trousers like other people.

The family—Kerna took to calling the Maybecks

"the family" and we picked it up—was involved in a lot of theatricals at that time. Wallen was really pushed into being a little "actor." They had theatricals and plays at the Hillside Club; everybody acted. Maybeck had built the first building, and then it burned down and John White built the one that is there now. But it always had a theater, and everybody was in all kinds of plays, acting and singing and dancing. I did that too. Everybody did. The whole membership was always doing those things.

Wallen got along just fine with his father. He and Ben were very companionable. They trusted each other and helped each other. Mrs. Maybeck was another thing; she was always trying to lay down the law, and Wallen was beginning to make laws for himself. He believed the only sin was hurting other people. She would never listen to him. That caused a division in their philosophies when we were first married. Wallen was always trying to tell his mother what he and I had found together—that we didn't think it was wrong to drink, that we liked to give parties and have cocktails, that I used lipstick. Such horrible things as that! She was against it, and she wouldn't listen to him. It made him quite...not exactly unhappy, but he wanted to be able to talk to his mother the way my brother and I could talk to our mother. We didn't talk to our father but we did talk to our mother.

The Maybecks' big house burned in the fire of 1923. I was down on campus, in an upstairs classroom. We students were taking notes and listening, and it began to be very strange colors outside the window. It was a hot day in September. We began to look outside and we discovered that there was a fire. Everybody was let out of classes and began to mill around on campus. I don't know when I found Flo, but that afternoon we met and joined a group to do whatever we could to help. We were asked to come in the evening and make coffee and sandwiches for the fraternity boys who were trying to save the houses at Northgate, at Euclid and Hearst. They were up on the roofs with firehoses and wet blankets, and when they came down we'd offer them coffee and sandwiches.

People were coming down from the hills, toward the campus, because it had green grass. They went to the Campanile; there were more people all the time carrying a canary bird in a cage, the only thing they'd saved, or a whole bundle of laundry, the last thing they'd picked up. It was very exciting, and very sad. The whole hill, you know, was smoking and burning behind them.

I heard from Wallen that evening, and he said he and his father came home from work on the ferry at five o'clock, and coming toward Berkeley they saw all this smoke and fire and flames. They had nothing left but the clothes they stood up in. Mrs. May-beck was at the house up here. Kerna was there, in the afternoon, when the fire started, and she was wise enough to grab a satchel with all the deeds of the land, because this was their living, and so I always say she took the satchel with the deeds on one hand and her grandmother under her arm—Bloomie, Mrs. Maybeck's mother, was up there for the day, I don't know why—anyway, she took her grandmother and a bundle of deeds and they all rushed down to campus to the green grass and safety.

Then the family moved down into a little apart-ment on Henry Street, with Bloomie. Wallen couldn't stand it and came up to the ruin of the old house. He found that the floor, the cement floor of his workshop, was intact, and he swept it off and put his sleeping bag down and began to live there. Then the family sent up a couple of carpenters and they built the Studio around him.

They built a frame and they covered it with sacks dipped in pink bubblestone. Ben had met Mr. John Rice, the inventor of bubblestone, and they liked to experiment. There must have been frame walls, and they just dipped the sacks in pink bubblestone and hung them on the walls, or nailed them. That made a very quick and easy wall, and it's lasted fifty years!

41

"It's lasted fifty years." The Studio, as it looks today.

They experimented with bubblestone in the Mobilized Women's building on Shattuck Avenue. They tried all sorts of things. They made a very sculptural piece into the doors of the Christian Science Church on Dana Street. I think they were working about this time in Glen Ellen, because they made a whole little cottage of bubblestone up there, a resort dining room. Mr. Rice's son was here last September and he took me out to see a roof of bubblestone on a house below the Arlington. It's still there!

The Studio became a very beautiful place. They built that great big fireplace there, like mine here at 2751, only it has a huge concrete hood that you can see because the slope of that roof allows you to. Mine you can't see, because the slope of my roof doesn't allow you to. That fireplace in the Studio is very impressive.

With Wallen up here, Ben and Mrs. Maybeck didn't want to stay down on Henry Street, so they bought a little cottage, which was a real estate office, and they had it put on a truck and brought up to the tennis court, above the Studio, which was the only flat place on the hill. They moved it there and they had a living room and a little coffee alcove, which Ben loved because he could sit and have coffee and doughnuts and look out at everything that was happening on the hill.

The Cottage had a bathroom, and it had a sort of little built-in kitchen, a sink and an oven-stove arrangement, by the coffee place. Then they built a back porch which became their sleeping porch. It had a roof but no sides.

The last year of college I lived up at the Maybeck Studio. That year my brother came down to college, and Kerna was in New York. She had rolled out of college. Wallen and I were still very good friends, and Mrs. Maybeck invited my brother and me to occupy the Studio with him. So Peter and Wallen had one half of it, as it were, and I had the top bedroom and bathroom, which was Kerna's little end.

Ben and Mrs. Maybeck liked young people. They liked having us around. Mrs. Maybeck did the cooking in the Cottage every night, and every night we ate with them. Then, when we got through with dinner she piled up the dishes and we washed them. They liked having us around. Thursday nights they would come down to the Studio and visit, and listen to the symphony on the radio.

Jaime de Angulo, the eccentric anthropologist who lived right above at 2815 Buena Vista Way, used to come down and listen to the symphony sometimes. He once showed us the gaits of the horse, how the legs moved when the horse ran. But we were a little too young to interest him very much.

44

I was still there, in the Studio with my brother, when I graduated; I graduated from there. That was in 1927; Wallen and I got married in September of that year. I thought about it all very seriously. I guess I always knew in my heart I would marry Wallen, right from the time I first met him. But I also felt that I had to have a little experience in the meantime, and also sort of prove to myself that I could attract other men.

Wallen was a kidder, and he was full of little quips, or little jokes, and *puns!* Oh, he made puns! He had a dry sense of humor. He made music, he sang; later he had an armadillo mandolin which we got in Mexico, bought it from a man.

I guess I went up to the ranch for a while, and then came down to meet Flo, and we went on the train and stayed in her house in Oregon. I got a job in a store there. Because I didn't rightly know what I wanted to do. Wallen and I would write each other, and finally I decided I'd marry him, but I didn't want to get married in Portland, Oregon.

My mother had a very good friend in Vancouver, B.C., and I decided to ask her if I could come up there, which I did. I just got on a bus, and went up there, and wrote Wallen where I was, and then he came up in the old Packard. We got married from there.

We didn't tell our parents. My mother knew what

I was doing; my father wasn't there. Neither Wallen nor I wanted to stir up the Maybecks, because it would be like putting a stick in an ant nest, and so we thought this was our own business, and we'd just go up if we wanted to and get married. We got married very nicely, in the Episcopal Church, with this family of Nyes as our attendants. Mrs. Nye had a daughter my age, that was one reason I went up. I had known her from the first days with Uncle Nick in Mill Valley, and we had kept in touch with each other.

So after Wallen and I were married we got into the car and took the car ferry to Vancouver Island, to Nanaimo, and spent our first night in the Empress Hotel, which was a romantic thing to do— a great big wonderful place. I've been back since and I wouldn't think it was very exciting now. It's over-*run* with tourists! But then it was quiet, with a few people around, and very orderly, and you were beautifully waited on—no matter who you were. It was very, very nice, very English. They served tea every afternoon in the parlor. Traveling English people would come into the lobby carrying their portable bathtubs!

Then we put on old clothes and took the car and camped all the way down to Berkeley, along the coast. My brother was still here and Kerna was still here, and we all lived in the Studio. Then we began to build the old garage into a little house, and that's the Cubby House.

Ben in front of the Cottage.

Five

The Cubby House, The Twins

The Cubby House grew out of the big old garage of the family house which had burned down in 1923. It was on La Loma, just past Buena Vista, and it had an entrance on the old county road that ran all the way up to the corner where the Temple of the Wings is now. The Maybecks had sold all that land where the Temple of the Wings is from the La Loma Park piece; they got ten thousand dollars for it, and that was the money they used to buy the two thousand acres up on Pine Ridge. (When they sold that land for the same price they paid for it all they got was me!) That dirt road was used by horses and wagons to carry lumber up the hill. It must have turned and gone on toward Grizzly Peak.

It was Mr. and Mrs. Boynton who built the Tem-

ple of the Wings. It was supposed to be a Greek
Temple. Mrs. Boynton was a dancer in the style of
Isadora Duncan—they said she had gone to school
with Isadora Duncan. The Temple had a central
hall, and two curved wings on either side, with
thirty-two tall, tall pillars holding up the roof. It
was very beautiful. The Boyntons lived there, without any walls, just canvas curtains that let down in
bad weather.

After a while the Boyntons decided it was too cold
in the Temple of the Wings without any walls, and
so they inserted a house between the pillars. It was
wonderfully designed. The pillars became part of
the rooms. One can be seen in the wall of the bathroom.

Mrs. Boynton taught all the young Berkeley girls
to dance. Her daughter, Sülgwynn and her son Durvol were also dancers. Sülgwynn taught in Berkeley
private schools.

The Boyntons were vegetarians, and they ate a
lot of nuts and dried fruit. They used to send their
children to school with lunches of nuts and dried
fruit, and the children would try to exchange their
nuts for other children's baloney sandwiches.

The whole area up here was called Nut Hill, in
those days. Maybe it was because of the Boyntons,
or maybe there were nut orchards up here.

The Cubby House was a long, low building, about

eighty feet long and twenty feet wide, because it accommodated the big Packard—and anyway they always built very large. It had four-foot overhang eaves, and it was built on this little drive, so that the car had access from the dirt road onto it, and we had access out of it onto that same level to the Studio. We lived in the Studio and we worked on the Cubby House, and what we did was to utilize the four-foot overhangs. We put the walls out that far, and we put a little bathroom—a toilet and basin—in one corner, and then, after some time, we utilized them again and put in a stove and a drain board and the sink, and that was the kitchen.

Much later I put in a little fireplace to steady the place down, and also to block water from running into it. On the other side of the room was another overhang, and into that we put cabinets and closets and a couch. That was a sleeping area. We broke this long room in half by a partition that moved so we could have our dining table near the kitchen and, after they were born, we could have the twins' beds and our bed in the other end, near the bathroom. It really worked very well, and of course our entrance was French doors; it had lots of light coming in. There were windows over the kitchen end, but no skylights. Never heard of skylights. We must have worked on it a year.

It was when we were working on the Cubby

House that Kerna, who was helping me, complained that I wasn't as vigorous about working as I had been. I began to slow down. I hadn't thought one way or another about it particularly, and then I sort of realized—although I knew very little about anything like this—that I must be pregnant. Mrs. Maybeck noticed that I was slowing down, and Kerna said, "Don't blame her, she's pregnant." I think that was the first that Mrs. Maybeck knew of it. When I first knew I was pregnant I didn't tell her about it; I didn't think it was anybody's business. I was very absorbed in my own predicament, and how I was going to handle it. Where we could go. I didn't want to have the baby here, so we went to Marin County. We rented a little house, called the Robin's Nest, in San Anselmo. Then we moved to Larkspur. My cousins Paul and Thea were living across the street. I was pregnant there the last couple of months, and did a *great* deal of walking all over Marin County.

Nobody knew I had twins until they were born! Being pregnant made a difference in the way we lived, but not very much, because I remember the twins were born the tenth of March, and on New Year's day we went to a great big party in San Francisco, and we all walked down Market Street, me too, singing and jumping around and so forth.

On March tenth we rushed to the hospital in Ross. I had a big front window. I think they had about four or five women who were pregnant. It was a small hospital, but I had a room with an Italian woman who came in after me, and here I was struggling along, and having a very long labor, and she just came in and went into labor, and came out with a ten-pound baby! With black hair. I was absolutely appalled.

Finally I went into real labor and then they realized that there was a blockage, nothing was happening, and the doctor took Andriana (Cherry for short), the first baby, with instruments, and then Sheila followed, and I remember either the doctor or Wallen saying, "My God, there are two of them!" Then I passed out and I woke up in my little bed, and they told me I had two babies. I said, "That's wonderful, because we'll give one to Thea." She was the cousin across the street. She was trying to get pregnant, and she wanted a baby very much. None of it was real to me. Then of course I got to like them!

We wired the family in Los Angeles, where Ben was working on a big house for Earl C. Anthony, and we said "We had twins!! Two for the price of one!" They answered, "Hooray, stop, hooray, stop."

The twins were so cute! No, they weren't cute, they were just beautiful, perfect little carvings! They weighed about five and a half pounds. They were very small. But they were perfect in every way,

"We had twins! Two for the price of one!"

you know, they were really beautiful, perfect babies. So Thea immediately got pregnant herself, she got so excited about my babies. And that's Teddy, who ended up going to college, with Cherry, here. Now she's an architect in Crockett.

I always went all summer to the ranch, because my father had to go out to work, and my mother couldn't be left alone up there, ten miles from town. They had never had a car. I had to go up and be with her, and so I just picked up the babies and I went. We bought a little car called Topsy Dodge for fifty dollars. Wallen would come up, as soon as he got out at five o'clock on Friday. He'd just get in the Packard and rush up, and come down again, Monday, early. It didn't seem so far, but it was far, though, boy was it far!

But we enjoyed the ranch; we had all sorts of projects; we worked on the road, widening it, taking out curves. We cut wood, and stacked it up for the winter; we made a little swimming hole for the twins. We did a lot of reading and writing. My mother wrote her sisters in Holland a lot, kept up that end of things.

We'd get so hot in the summer, absolutely red hot, that all activity would stop. Everybody would take a long deck chair and stretch out with a book, until the sun went over the hill and things would cool off.

A lunch on the road. Left to right: Wallen and the dog, Little Grannie with a twin, Jacomena, Kerna with a twin, Ben and the Packard.

And we had sprinklers going all the time in the garden.

Even before we married we had gone up there. We made improvements, which often my father demolished when he came home. My mother and I built stone gate posts at the end of the road where you entered the flat area of the yard. We took wheelbarrows and we collected the rocks and we bought cement and we had a level. Then we got those rods that have a place for a hinge, and we stuck those in before the cement was hard, and we had a gate, so that stray cattle couldn't get into our garden. And they're still there!

Then Wallen and I decided to come back from Mill Valley and live in Berkeley. The Maybecks were still in Los Angeles where Ben was doing the house for Mr. Anthony. He got very sick down there; he had surgery on his prostate and something went wrong. He was very sick and spent his time lying in the sunshine drinking water and eating vegetables. So he got well again.

When our babies were four months old we moved into the Cottage. Kerna was in the Studio; my brother was still there, finishing up his senior year. We all ate together—we had a black woman— I think she was black—really Little Grannie (as we now called her), hired her to take care of Kerna. But what she did was cook for all four of us in the Cottage, and all she knew how to cook was spaghetti. It was awful, it was simply awful; all of us were a little under the weather, and we should have had really wonderful cooking, but we didn't; we had this miserable stuff she cooked. Everything she cooked was soggy. Gad! And I was like a wilted rose. I had no energy whatsoever, and I was nursing the babies. We were sleeping in a little bedroom we made by closing in the porch behind the living room of the Cottage. Kerna would come up and we would sit in back where we had cleared a little bit of land. We'd bring the babies out there in their baskets, and we would lie there on blankets and pillows and read and talk and drink tea, nurse the babies. Spend the whole summer that way, just doing nothing.

Wallen was working; he went right on just doing what he always did. It didn't cost us very much to live. We managed fine. I guess we all threw in a little bit; Kerna probably did too. Peter, my brother, didn't have any money. He was just getting through that last year. I guess we probably went to the Farmer's Market and bought cheap vegetables, and just, you know, lived *very,* very simply. The Chinese vegetable man would come in his truck and we could buy eggs and milk and vegetables from him, and later I had a laundry man, but I don't think I had then. But I might have, because things were awfully reasonable; everything was cheap and easy.

The family wanted to see the babies. When they came home we had to get out of the Cottage, and this house, 2751, wasn't built yet, so we scrambled around and fixed up the Cubby House. We were still living there when the twins were walking around, and they would go up every morning to see Little Grannie and Ben at the Cottage and have their breakfast up there. From La Loma to the Cottage there was a little path under the plum trees, and they would knock on the door and say, "Can both of me come in?" The family loved to have them. I was sort of out of it and wanted to sleep late, and I knew they were safe over there. But Little Grannie got a little much of them and she put a chicken wire fence around the Cubby House. They just clambered right over.

Ruth Pennell, across the street, once told me that somebody knocked on the door and she opened it and two little people three years old said, "We is coming to wisit." They had stuffed their feet into my high-heeled shoes and clopped over the street.

Then in 1929 the family decided that they would build two houses, this one at 2751 Buena Vista, and one at 2780 Buena Vista, the same design as this one, only below the road. When these two houses were finished, which took a while, we each moved into a good home. The family moved to 2780. Kerna

59

Ben and Annie Maybeck and a twin.

Piet van Huizen, Ben Maybeck and the twins.

wasn't married yet; she lived in her sorority, I suppose—or she lived with the family up here, sometimes. We lived here in 2751.

We began to be much more presentable people.
They had a good house; we had a good house. We
could invite our friends up here. We had made a lot
of friends on the campus when Peter and I were
there. Kerna was around; we had lots of parties at
the Studio. Kids liked coming up on the hill. They
were all getting married and having children; the
parties became much more subdued, much more
family style.

Then the twins, when they got to be old enough,
went down to Hillside School.

The Angulos lived up above, so we didn't see them
very much. Ben and Jaime de Angulo were friendly,
and they saw a lot of each other. I think they
exchanged poetry, and they helped each other with
tiles for the house. The Angulos had drunken parties and we laughed about them; we thought it was
awfully funny because drunken Indians would
occasionally roll down the hill, and we thought that
was very funny.

At this time Ben was working on Principia, that
big college in St. Louis, Missouri. That went on
some five years. They had a house there, on the
bluff. But they would come back here, and then go

"They had a good house, we had a good house."
Twenty-seven fifty-one Buena Vista as it looks today.

back there. We often took them down to the train. Little Grannie had a beautiful wine-colored woolen suit, a two-piece suit that she bought—or maybe Kerna bought it for her. It had a long skirt and jacket that matched. I remember her getting on the train in it, and looking very well.

Little Grannie was very vigorous, interested in everything, in the plans Ben made, the people he met, the people he was going to meet, the people he needed to meet, where the plans should go, who was going to pay for what. She was a business genius. She took care of all the money. Ben couldn't keep track of a nickel! Ben was so charming and so generous that if he met anybody he liked he would give them something. He began to have everything I had on the dining table covered with silver! Little Grannie found out about that, and put a quick stop to it.

I liked her. I liked parts of her very much. I liked her sense of humor. I could rise right up to it. We could go back and forth with jokes, and laugh and laugh.

Six

Hilltop, the War

When the twins were in the first grade we decided we wanted to get away from just the family all the time. You know, this was a very in-grown family—all these members, everybody depending on each other, seeing each other all the time, carrying around each other's packages. So we decided, let's go and stay somewhere else for a while. I went to Ross in the Packard—we called it Packy—with a friend of mine, Wendy. We went to a real estate person who told us where there were possible rentals and we found a big two story Victorian house on San Anselmo Road. It was about four blocks from the train station; that was nice for Wallen. It had eight redwood trees in the backyard, a little stream running through it, two enormous cherry trees in the

*"We called it Packy." On the way to the ranch
one Thanksgiving.*

front yard, and roses all around underneath. A rose garden, a real rose garden! And a hedge on each side. Of course we were enchanted with all this. We rented it for twenty-five dollars a month.

The twins were in the first grade of school, about five. They would walk five or six blocks down a level road to San Anselmo School. They went to school, and Wallen hopped onto the inter-urban train to the city, which met the ferry in Sausalito. It was easier for him than Berkeley had been. I was left to my own devices. I did a lot of writing and painting at that time, nothing very worthwhile, but I did it, because I just wanted to express myself. I had two or three friends, and I did a great deal of walking. I also did a great deal of reading. It was lovely weather—and those cherry trees! First they were in full bloom and then they were full of cherries. I did a lot of gardening and working out in the garden pulling weeds and making it look nice, and just enjoying myself, my house and my garden. The kids would come home from school, then Wallen would come home, and we'd have dinner and on weekends maybe we'd go out to the beach, to Stinson and places like that. Of course the twins picked up dearest friends in the neighborhood, but I didn't. I really didn't find any people that I felt close to. I had all those friends in Berkeley, from college, but they were *there*. I'd been so close to Wendy, and suddenly she was in Berkeley and I was in Marin County.

But we didn't stay there; we went through the spring and the next winter. We rented it when it was raining, so that was spring, and the following winter the man who owned the house, who was a gardener, fell out of a tree when he was working and hurt his back badly. He couldn't get insurance if he had our rent coming in; he had to prove that he had no extra income and then they would support him. So he wanted his house back. Of course this was a crisis, and naturally we said we'd get out in a minute. So we came home and said, "What are we going to do? We need our house," 2751, because the family always said that was our house. "We really want our house back. What are we going to do?"

Ben and Little Grannie were living in 2751. Kerna had gotten married and was living in 2780 with Chick. So what to do? Well, Ben said, "You're wet and we're dry, and we don't want to move out of here, we're very comfortable. But we'll give you a piece of land, up on Hilltop Road. We've got lots of land up there." And so we said, "All right."

I was up at the ranch, as usual, that summer, coming and going, and Wallen found us a place where we could come back to live, an apartment on Solano Avenue, above a butcher shop and a grocery, and the twins loved it! They could go down the stairs and prowl around in the grocery store and they'd be given baloney and cookies. We had a bed-room looking out over the street. The inter-urban trains ran down Solano Avenue; every twenty min-utes a train came either up or down, going to the city or coming away from the city. I didn't sleep for a week. And then all of a sudden I didn't hear them anymore.

The twins started school, Thousand Oaks School. They came in late, so they had to be in different rooms, and they weren't used to being separated. Sheila got along fine, but Cherry would wake up in the morning with a pain in her stomach and say she didn't want to go to school. That went on for a while until I talked it over with my doctor, who said, "You'd better get them together. There's nothing the matter with this child except she doesn't want to go to school to a strange room by herself." So I talked to the teacher, and she said, "We're so crowded we don't have another desk in Sheila's room, but I'll take Cherry with me at noon and see that she plays with Sheila and the other children from my room." They got along fine after that.

The twins were cute; they had bobbed hair, Dutch bob, and I always bought them the same dresses and the same coats but they didn't always wear them at the same time, because they didn't want to be mixed up. But they always went together. (One day, when they were small, they had new lacy petti-

"The twins were cute."

coats, and they put them on and they marched down to Hillside School, in just their lovely little lacy white petticoats. The teacher brought them home! But they were as well-dressed, then, in their petticoats, as children are today in their expensive little dresses.)

I made them all their clothes. They had a minimum of clothes. We didn't believe in overdressing or over-supplying them with toys, either. They didn't seem to need them anyway. And then as they grew older they wanted more clothes, and I said I would make them, and I would wash them, but they'd have to iron them themselves. Because they would change their clothes three times a day! You know, have another pretty new dress on, in the afternoon. A little later, when they were going to El Cerrito High School, they wanted lots of clothes, and they had lots of clothes. This grew into their wanting formals, and they also wanted lots of formals.

Wallen got them mixed up every so often. I always thought I could tell them apart. I got them mixed up on the telephone a few times. In general I just knew. They were used to people not knowing which was which.

To me there was a difference in their temperaments. I think Cherry was more aggressive; Sheila was more abiding. She was always very helpful and soft, caring. Cherry was very lively. Cherry would push Sheila into a room if there were people there and Sheila was shy. They were so alike, and they were so much one person. They had no rivalry. They always said, "Both of me."

That fall of course we would go up all the time to where they were building our house on Hilltop. We were excited about the Hilltop plans. All that lovely land! We went up every weekend. We raked and we cut grass. Then we dug a dirt road from the end of the street, Purdue Avenue. We made a long street to the top of our acre. From there we looked east over the brushy canyon to green hills, far away. To the west the whole Bay Area was spread before us. (I used to lie on the couch in the bay window, when the house was done, and watch the drama of storms, winds and rain.) I laid a lot of brick in the little patio and the wall around it. The twins made friends in the neighborhood. New Year's Eve of 1938 we moved in; we spent our first night there. We moved into one wing of the house. We put in the garage right away, so that we would have a closed-in patio. We lived in that one wing of the house until they finished the big living room with the big fireplace.

All that time everybody was working, all doing something on the house. Ben would walk over his sheepskin coat and supervise—three miles. I don't know how old he was then, but he wasn't young at

"It was a challenging place to live!" Hilltop as it looks today.

all; he was retired. He never learned to drive; neither did Little Grannie. They always found boys who could drive for them. And of course we did too.

They had given us two acres. We sold one acre for four thousand dollars and we built the house on the other acre for that money. We were cutting corners. We were finding all the cheapest materials possible. We prefabricated panels for the living room, and did all the brick work ourselves. We did everything we could ourselves. Wallen did the wiring, and the quickest and cheapest roof was corrugated iron—a barn roof, fireproof. The windows were factory glass windows.

It was a challenging place to live! Winds blew, fog flowed in, sun brought grass and China lilies from the earth. It was a good-for-the soul kind of place. It was a beginning house for us. Now it's finished, beautifully lived in and cared for by its new owners and it gets its picture in magazines.

It was while we were living at Hilltop that this house, 2751, had a fire. Little Grannie and Ben were still living here. One day I came to 2751 and there was a crowd of people in the street and the fire department was here, and Little Grannie was running around. The house was burning! There were firemen on top of the roof; they had chopped a hole in it and were flooding the house with water.

Actually none of the timbers in the construction

of the house were damaged. They were only browned, like a piece of toast. It had started from some french fried potatoes Little Grannie was cooking on the stove. She had gone down to talk to the Mayor about a road, and forgotten to turn them off. When she got back and saw the fire she tried to rush in, but a policeman said, "Lady, you can't go in there." She said, "I can too; that's my fire, that's my house." She wanted to get some deeds and papers and things out. But nothing like that was destroyed in the house. Only just the roof panels, which were scorched and had to be removed, and the rafters, which were all fine but had lost about a quarter of an inch of wood, and the glass in the windows, which all had burst out. And the floor was very badly blackened. I never could remove it. I tried scraping, I tried strong detergents, I tried painting it. It's just the way it wants to be, very dark brown and mellow. It's a honey maple floor that has been *over*-kiln dried. It's very shiny, just from usage, I think. We wash it with soap and water quite often.

Nothing needed to be repaired of the structure. Just the paneling. Little Grannie and Ben got sand-blasters in here and they took the carbon off all the woodwork. Then Ben and Little Grannie began to replace the burnt pieces between the rafters. That was white pine, knotty pine, and it's very fragile and dry. That had really burned, so they had car-

Twenty-seven fifty-one after the sandblasting.

penters build a scaffold and the carpenters would go up and measure every single space separately, because they're not a standard size. They had college boys helping them, too, and Wallen and whoever else.

The charred part goes down the stairs and hits two doors down there, that's all. That's as far as it went. It didn't go in my room, it didn't go in any of the other rooms. It just scorched the railing and the stairs. But those stairs are inch-thick oak, and they could stand a quarter of an inch loss by sandblasting. Ben and Little Grannie lived here all the time the house was being transformed, getting its face lifted, as it were. We were up on Hilltop.

We didn't live there very long, because in 1941 Wallen was drawn into the war; he was a reserve officer. In July of that year he was drafted; he went into the Signal Corps, which was telephone work, and he lived at Hamilton Field.

When war was declared I was down at the Hillside Club practicing a play, and Wallen phoned in so I could relay it to all the people there: We're at war. Pearl Harbor had happened. It was very dramatic, very scary.

By that time we were already having blackouts. Ben and Little Grannie had gone up to Twain Heart and rented this little house, because they had no boys to drive the car anymore. All the boys had gone, and we were way up there on Hilltop.

After Pearl Harbor away went Wallen, and pretty soon we went too, because we couldn't stay up there on Hilltop by ourselves. The army had brought up about ten of those little portable shacks, little cabins, with numbered boards and you bolt them together. (Kerna and I bought one, later on, and that's the store room behind the Cottage.) They had one of those circulating lights—no guns, just those lights—but there were a lot of soldier boys stationed up there and with the twins it wasn't a good place for us. I stayed at Hilltop as long as possible, but in February of 1942 we moved over to Hamilton Field too, the twins and I, because Wallen had got a house for us.

In June he was ordered to Salt Lake City, but there was no housing there, so I went up to the ranch with the twins. We couldn't stay at Hamilton Field because our man was gone; the wives and children were not allowed to stay without the officer.

At the ranch we had our usual lovely summery time, wearing practically no clothes, and gardening and walking and playing with cats and dogs and twins and having lovely days. As soon as we could of course we followed Wallen, after he found a house in Salt Lake City.

I guess we must have driven there in the car! Did

I drive the twins from the ranch to Salt Lake City? I suppose so. Anyway, we got there. We had the car, and we had this little house with a little garden in back. It was *very* dirty. There was a big coal mine south of Salt Lake City and all the windows and window trim and every wood surface had a *slight* film of coal dust on it. It was amazing to me; it made me not want to touch anything. There were lovely parks to walk in, but for the first time in my life I saw garbage cans on the sidewalk; you could see them as you walked down the street. It was very disgusting to me. They appeared once a week, and then they went back in the gardens again.

We had all our goods and chattels stored away somewhere, and so we had to make do with all kinds of funny things. We ran out of clothes and we had to buy and make a few. We made friends with the neighbor children, of course; we all played in the back yard. But it was a period of nothingness for me because I had to stay with the children. I couldn't do much exploring; they were a little too young for that. So we waited for the next jump. And the next jump was to New Mexico.

This time Wallen was with us, and we all drove to New Mexico in the Packard. We had never seen this kind of country. We began to see desert country, and the kind of homes that people live in in hot countries. We finally got to the Rio Grande River—I don't remember the name of the town—but it was very foreign and very different, very Spanish, Mexican, and then we had to drive down south along the river to come to the place called Alamagordo.

In Salt Lake City, when we learned Wallen was going to be moved to Alamagordo, which was just building up as an air base, we asked some of the officers who had come flying back from there what it was like. They said, "Well, it's nothing! There's just nothing there!" Well, we hadn't known if we wanted to go, but we didn't want to be left behind, so we ventured forth into New Mexico. And fell in love with the place, for some strange reason. Sun and wind and enormous skies, and those adobe houses.

So we came to Alamagordo. It was a small town, about four thousand people. There was a main street, New York Street, and on one side of that street the Anglos lived, in *maybe* wooden houses, and on the other side of the street the Mexicans lived in adobe houses. They had little gardens. We couldn't find a house, because the Air Force had landed there, on their air strip, and also in the town. We lived in a motel, and we ate all our meals out. That was a new experience too; you got to eat the same thing over and over because that was what they had. A lot of things we didn't like, very strong Mexican things that made me cry.

Then I found a four-room cottage, with a screen

porch along the sidewalk, for twenty-five dollars a month. That included cockroaches. We soaked the little house in Clorox, bought a bed and a sofa and a chair in a second hand store, hung some fine Indian rugs about and settled down. Christmas came and everyone sang "White Christmas" day and night. Everyone was very homesick.

The girls went to school. The school was half English and half Spanish. The girls made friends. The main thing that was happening in the town was the U.S.O., especially the dances twice a week for the town girls and boys on the base. On Wednesday night and Friday night, I think, there was a band and the boys were bussed into town, and the girls all walked over to the U.S.O., and I went with the twins, of course. I had to chaperone them. Anyway, even *I* danced, because women were so scarce. I think maybe there were a hundred girls in the town, including me. There were endless supplies of boys. We danced our feet off. We had a marvelous time. At eleven o'clock the officers came with the jeeps and they swept the boys up and took them back to the base. These dances were very exciting things for the town. It really turned everybody upside down. All kinds of things happened.

The Spanish people didn't come to the dances. If they were Air Force, yes, but mostly these Air Force boys were from Detroit. If the Mexican boys—they were not Mexican, they were called Spanish-American, you never called them Mexican—were in the Air Force, of course they came too. The girls were anything that was female. Local Spanish-American girls, American girls, everybody, everybody. And some of the wives of the young men who were on the base. All kinds of people. We had a marvelous time.

The base was getting built up; and there were lots of soldiers there, Air Force personnel and officers. Wallen had his office, and it had an orange crate for a desk. It was a very temporary building, sort of oval shaped, a quonsut hut. The whole place was in a state of construction.

Sometimes Saturday there were picnics, U.S.O. picnics.

Then Wallen was made officer in charge of Riodoso; Riodoso was forty-five miles away; it was up in the mountains in the pine trees, and it was a little tiny pioneer town. Wallen was in charge of the soldiers camped there; they could go up there and be cool, and there were also slot machines and there were places to dance and there were places to eat, and there were fights. Wallen had the largest man in the whole Air Force as policeman for the main street, and he saw to it that they didn't have fights, and that they were polite to people. I remember that boy, and what a good time he had klunking heads together if the boys started to fight.

Well, we spent our evenings in these little…I guess they were bars; that was all there was there. Everybody went to the bars; the bars were wide open. They were very good ones. There wasn't much trouble. Anyway, we would go up there weekends, as much as we could.

I made some friends in Alamagordo. The doctor and the minister were the two people that had really nice houses in Alamagordo, and so they entertained quite a lot, and everybody knew them and admired them. I made friends with the doctor's wife, Margorie and that friendship lasted for years and years. In fact I went three times to visit Margorie when she moved to Spain from America.

Margorie was Jewish, from New York, and she was sophisticated and very womanly. She never wore slacks. She always wore dresses and skirts. She was a *lady!* She had come out of the brownstone houses of New York, where her mother always had a maid in the house, and so she herself always had a maid, even in Alamagordo, absolutely!

What drew me to her was the fact that she was sophisticated, and she was from a lot of places, and she was very friendly toward me. I liked Rudy, her husband, too; they were intelligent people, they had music and books, and they were a real magnet in this town of four thousand people, roughly half of them Spanish, and the other half who knows what kind of people, who lived by their radios.

New Mexico was magic. We drove up to Taos on our G.I. gas and stayed at Taos Inn. Indians waited on our table and took care of our room. The cottonwoods that lined the main street were golden. The air was golden too, and smelled of sweet cedar smoke from the little fireplaces in the adobe homes. There was a gallery opening somewhere every Saturday night, to see the paintings. It seemed as though everyone painted or wrote and made music. You began to hear stories about people—always changing, this way, that way. Not much money anywhere, but so much energy and fun, too.

That ended of course when Wallen was finally shipped out of there to Springfield, Ohio. We went with him; we weren't going to be left behind. We just packed up and left, and we left with great regret. We had such interesting and good times in Alamagordo!

Wallen during the War.

Seven

Following Wallen

We went to Springfield, Ohio, and we went from summer sunshine, and dancing every night, to snow and a German, tight-up community. And nothing for me to do except stoke the furnace and go down with a basket and buy groceries the way the other women did.

The girls went to school, and of course made friends. It was cold and rainy and snowy and we kept our furnace going so hard that it dried the wallpaper off the walls. We were used to warmth, and this was very hard for us. There wasn't anything to do. I tried to volunteer for the U.S.O., but there was nothing happening there. I went to the Officer's Club in Springfield and it was absolutely deadly dull, so I stayed home most of the time and

87

read and made a few paintings, and so forth. But it didn't last so very long, perhaps four months, and then fortunately we had to leave.

We went with Wallen again, in our old car, which did not have windshield wipers, across the Alleghenies from Columbus, Ohio to Fort Monmouth, New Jersey. We passed through snow storms and then we came to Gettysburg and looked at that, and then Yorktown. Finally we got to the Atlantic Ocean at Longbranch, New Jersey. There we found an apartment on the upper story of a very old but very charming Victorian house, owned by two old ladies who were very kind to us. Again the girls were put in school, and again Wallen went to the base, and again I had nothing to do.

It was beautiful country. We were about two blocks away from the ocean, the Atlantic, and on weekends we would go and sit on the beach, which was a very steep beach. The water got very deep immediately, so it wasn't too good for swimming. There were big houses, twenty-eight room houses, Victorians, built on the cliffs or high plateaus above the ocean, and these were occupied by Jewish people from New York who came out weekends just to be in the country.

There were beautiful flat roads with white pebbles, sort of white, sandy pebbles, and there were places where they were raising horses, race horses. There were big flat areas with white board fences and big houses, and they'd have a couple of horses in the meadow. We did a lot of walking, and we kept saying, "When will spring come, when will spring come?" Because it was very cold. This was March. And they said, "Well, spring will come on the first of May, and that will be it. After that it gets terribly hot." So we looked forward to that one day of spring that had been promised us, but in the meantime we had beautiful bushes with blossoms all over the place, and trees began to burgeon out in green, light green, dark green, beautiful greens. I wrote a lot. I wrote my diary, I wrote about what I saw. I didn't see very much. I went to the Officer's Club once in a while. I didn't feel I would be there long enough to make relationships with people. The Aunties in the house were nice, and that was it.

The twins, I think, felt the same way. They had been so buoyant and adventurous up to now; now they didn't care whether they made friends or not. And I realized when Wallen was ordered on that we would have to go home, that it was time for the girls to have a home of their own. So when Wallen was suddenly ordered overseas to England we took the car, the old Packard, and taught the girls how to drive. They got their driver's licenses and when

Wallen took off, the girls and I packed up and left for California.

We went first to Washington D.C. and stayed with Aimee Holmquist, who was a friend from Berkeley. We stayed a week there, and it was terribly, terribly hot. Then we just got into the car and started west. It didn't occur to us that it was a sort of adventurous thing to do.

On the trip we always picked up soldier boys. Finally we got across the Mississippi and we picked up an older sailor, who was returning to Portland, Oregon, where he had a radio station. We liked him very much. He went the rest of the way home with us; we would go to a hotel at night, and he'd get a room at one end of the hotel, and we'd get rooms at the other, and we'd all meet at breakfast in the morning, and start out again. He did the driving, although I took turns too, but he did a great deal of the driving. In time we were in Utah. He had to go north to Portland, Oregon, and we had to continue west to Berkeley. So we had to say goodbye to him, but we certainly hated to. But he just got out of the car, somewhere at the crossroads, and he stood there with his thumb out till he got another ride. I'm sure he got there.

We went on then, past Salt Lake City, and gradually toward the California mountains, the Sierra Nevadas. This began to be sort of familiar country, and of course once we were past Tahoe and down the slope to the west coast we were in familiar territory. And we had a house to go to.

We got to Berkeley. We had been given gasoline by the Air Force, I think, *exactly* a certain number of gallons that would take us at forty-five miles an hour all the way to Berkeley. We weren't allowed to drive faster than fifty because that would use up our gasoline. So we finally got home; there was our house, empty, 2751 Buena Vista Way. And of course Berkeley was a little foggy, and a little smelling of eucalyptus trees, and the house was absolutely desolate looking, inside.

There had been people renting it, and they had an old green rag rug and Little Grannie's davenport, and there was a big table, and that was about all. Our furniture was stored in Antioch; it had been there all that time. We didn't get it back for a year; the Air Force didn't dispense it because Wallen wasn't here. Anyway, we couldn't get hold of it.

So what we did was to go to a furniture store and buy a davenport made out of three great big overstuffed tomato red chairs. We bought a great big white rug, too, a cotton-wooly kind of rug, and what with Little Grannie's davenport and new couch covers, that did us until Wallen came home.

We also bought a puppy, a blond cocker Spaniel. While I was away Margorie, the doctor's wife who was my friend in Alamagordo, got divorced. The doctor went to New Orleans on a medical conference, and left Margorie home. Well, by golly, he fell in love with somebody in New Orleans, a woman named Tookie. So we named our puppy Tookie after that woman.

We settled in in a kind of way. Anyway, we had beds; the twins had the twin beds in their room, and I had a great big bed in the south room, which was the happy room in the morning because the sun came in. The twins went back to school, and they began to have activities and friends. I went visiting in the neighborhood, picking up old friends. That was when Martin Cayman and Richard Skahen were renting the Studio. I saw Ruth Pennell, across the street, and her sons. We all got to be very good friends and everybody began to have dances on Saturday nights. And more and more of the men began to come home.

But Wallen couldn't come home. He didn't come home for a year. He'd been sent first to England, then to Paris. He made some friends in Paris, so it wasn't too bad. Then came the end of the war, the armistice! I remember we all went over to San Francisco and walked up Market Street, singing. They had bonfires on the street, with everybody jumping up and down, happy, happy, happy!

Then Wallen was sent to Frankfurt. He found us a house there in the E.J. Farben Compound, a village. That was the time of the U.S. occupation of Germany. Lots of American soldiers kind of putting Germany back together again and keeping order. The Nazis were gone, and the Nuremburg Trials had happened, and we had a jeep! We were given a jeep. There were no American cars in Frankfurt—later they began to come one by one. No color in Germany, nothing but snow and greyness.

But we began to find old friends tucked away here and there, also Air Force, or Occupation Forces. And we began to do all kinds of things and enjoy life quite a lot. We had an apartment—a house in a row of houses all attached to each other and five stories high. Each had a little tiny front porch made out of pipes, and a back porch. We had a little garden in the back. The Germans had raised their cabbages, broccoli, and lettuce there. That's about all we had. We ate out of that garden. We were glad to have the green stuff. We had our jeep and we went to the commissary for our groceries, which were very, very limited. You could get G.I. white bread, and you could get about five different kinds of canned vegetables, corned beef and tuna, canned butter from Denmark, and fresh milk. I guess we got dried milk to cook with.

The owner of the house was my housekeeper. She was allowed to live there if she worked for her keep. She had been two years in Berlin at the American College, so she spoke very good English. Her husband was a pharmacist in the E.J. Farben Pharmaceutical Company.

Oh, Germany! Well, we were there about a year, I guess. We went to a little village where the displaced people were collected. A friend of ours who was an officer was in charge of that section. These people had to be sorted out and sent back to wherever they came from. They were kind of lost—Germans, Jews, Russians, Poles, all kinds of people, kind of stranded there in Frankfurt. And the city itself, of course—there were piles of bricks, houses with half of it blown away; you could look into the rooms and there were bedsteads hanging there. It was a weird place. We couldn't drive through it.

We couldn't go into any of the German places, anyway. They had a concert hall and we wanted to go to a concert; we weren't allowed to go there. We were only allowed to go to places that had been explored to see that they were safe, that the roofs wouldn't fall in on us. And we were really not supposed to mix with Germans, or the Jewish people. But we did. Everybody did. Everybody traded books, everybody traded cigarettes for jewelry, or anything that was movable. G.I.'s took a lot of stuff. I traded

Frankfurt after the war.

three cartons of cigarettes for a beautiful amethyst ring.

We settled down to a very bucolic sort of life. We couldn't go very far because the snow was two feet deep. So we spent our free time in American bars and the Officers' Club.

The twins had all their time free. Every time they went to the Officers' Club it was full of soldiers. What was a romantic eighteen-year old to do but fall in love? Both Cherry and Sheila did. They were in a wonderland of admiration.

Then Wallen's tour of duty ended and we were given our orders to go home. During that last week Sheila got married, to Captain John Bathhurst. Cherry also had an attendant officer, but she didn't like him as well as Sheila liked Johnny. Johnny used to come down from Fitzlaar to Frankfurt on the autobahn. Then we got a chance to go skiing in Switzerland with an Air Force group. Cherry went with us but Sheila wouldn't go; she wanted to go to Fitzlaar and stay with Johnny, so we knew that this was serious. When we came back from the trip to Switzerland—which was beautiful and a lot of fun— we had a wedding for Sheila, in Fitzlaar, in a big cathedral. There were no flowers to be had anywhere in Germany, so she had a bouquet of green leaves that somebody had collected somewhere. They walked out under crossed bayonets. She had a little green suit, not a wedding dress. Anyway, we did the very best we could for her. And all those officers, and a great big reception, and a great big dinner, and everybody in Sunday dress uniforms, and we in the best clothes we had. We had gotten some blouses in Switzerland, silk blouses—I wish I had them now.

Then we had to leave, and the train came along, and everybody was in tears, Wallen, and Cherry, and I, and Sheila and Johnny on the platform, and our train chugged away.

Then we were stuck for a week in Bremerhaven. We got our ship in Bremerhaven. The bay was still full of mines, so you had to be very carefully ushered around. This was the Marine Jumper, and it was a very primitive ship. It had been built in Richmond, California, and there were thirty-five French brides on board. There were two thousand G.I.'s in the lower depths. The French brides were going home; they had married soldiers and were being shipped home to them, or carried along with them. All these G.I.'s were down in the hold, as it were, and we had cabins up in the upper decks. But there were fifty of us in a cabin. I had claustrophobia, so I had to get up every night and go to the door to the deck, and there was always a guard. The guard wouldn't let me out on the deck, but he'd let me stand in the doorway and breathe. So then, when I got cooled off

I'd go back to my bunk. There were three of us to a tier of bunks, one above the other.

There were very few girls on board, you can imagine. Cherry was practically *the* girl, and she was trailed day and night by groups of officers. There were no enlisted men on our deck. The officers had lovely cabins, and music, and I went there once or twice. But I really preferred sitting on the deck with those poor, seasick French brides.

So then we came back. I'm sure that we flew from New York—that we were sent to Fort Hamilton, and that we flew home from there. That was 1946.

Eight

Potting, Taos

When we got back from Germany there were a lot of people around that we knew. Sheila of course we had left in Germany, married, but Cherry was with us, and immediately settled down to go to college. Teddy van Loghem, the daughter of my cousin in San Anselmo, came and lived with us, here at 2751. Wallen went back to the phone company.

I had become interested in pottery in Germany. I looked at everything they were doing in the Special Services building, which was a sort of art center, and I found that pottery and clay were the only things that satisfied me at all. So when we went home, very shortly thereafter, they said, "Don't give it up, don't give it up."

The minute I got to Berkeley I inquired around

and heard that Edith Heath, who later had the famous Heath Pottery in Sausalito, was teaching a ceramics class in San Francisco. I went over, but soon I decided that I'd better get out of there. We were in a dark basement, and Edith soon left and we had a photographer for a teacher; we had no wheel and no kiln, and no good work was being done there.

I inquired around some more and I found that a man named Antonio Prieto was teaching at the California College of Arts and Crafts in Oakland. I went over there and I was so impressed with the work they were doing that I signed up as a student and began to work.

The people I met there became such good friends! Corkendall, Charles Fiske, Viola Frey and Noni Treadwell and others...I was there awfully long. I must have gone in 1946, and I didn't quit until 1978. I got a Master's degree in ceramics in 1952, and then I kept going there as an assistant. Then I began to be an instructor. I liked that, sure, but it wasn't as much fun as being a student. Because as a student you're so free! You can be working, doing your own work, and having the work go through the mill there, and know everybody, and be free. As a teacher you have to produce something for the students to listen to, and you have to teach them something. I didn't teach there very long, maybe five

Jacomena and Charles Fiske at the California College of Arts and Crafts. (Clay on the lense.)

years. I enjoyed it but I wasn't thrilled by it. I didn't feel like Viola, for instance, who came up in the system and kept blossoming into bigger and bigger things, a tremendous talent. I didn't do that. I plugged along and I was happy to be there, and glad I was making some money doing it. I enjoyed the students but it was a job now; before it had been just sheer pleasure, doing your own work, doing the best you knew, and creating your own stuff and making it better and better. As a teacher you weren't doing very much of that. You didn't have much time for yourself.

It was interesting to watch Viola, and also Peter Voulkos, who was there. He was a potter and he became a sculptor. He got his Master's in ceramics the same year I did. He was head of the U.C. ceramics department for a while. Then he went on from there, on his own, really, and began to do these strange things that he did, these people cut up and put together, big things. He would take ceramic tile, or sewer pipes, cut them in half, and stick them together in different ways. Then he went from that into metalwork. He got a big warehouse down on the waterfront in Emeryville and he began to work there in metal. He had a foundry down there. He had a couple of objects in San Francisco, near the police department, a great big thing made out of great big pipes.

I loved the early work he did; it was classical and beautiful. He could throw! He came from Montana, from a sheep farm, and he had studied in a tile factory somewhere, maybe Helena. He could throw a jar as high as two feet with a little tiny top. People would say, "What is that for?" He would say, "To hold wheat." You could put the seeds in one at a time. He used to sit and smoke a big cigar while he was throwing— so did Corkie—but he was a magnificent classical thrower. But there wasn't enough publicity in that.

I knew Antonio Prieto, who was head of the department. Corkendall and Charles Fiske were his assistants. I liked Tony Prieto's work very much. I bought several pieces and gave them away as presents. I never kept one myself ... well, I kept one little bowl. He was Spanish, Prieto, and he had a terrible temper. He could get very mad at people if they were sloppy or careless or untalented. He was a good friend if he liked you. He had a very nice wife, and four sons. The Prieto boys all did pottery too. Prieto went on to Mills College. He was the head potter there for quite a while and Corkendall took over his place at Arts and Crafts. While Prieto was at Mills, the great Japanese potter Rosanjin came through with boxes and boxes of pottery. He was going to have a show in New York; he had met one of the Rockefellers in Tokyo who had arranged all this. He stayed with us at my house for three days—with his interpreter, because he didn't speak any English.

Rosanjin's work was very strange. He owned a restaurant, a cafe, in Tokyo, and he wanted everyone to eat off beautiful dishes. So he began to make beautiful dishes. They were very strange and rough. I have a piece of his out there in the Pot Shop; it's square and it's dry like a piece of desert. He piled ashes here and there on it, which made round spots. I know I could sell it for over three hundred dollars. I don't know whether he thought dishes like that would be used in the restaurant. He may have made different things for that. He did glossy glaze ware too. He let us choose, and I chose this one. Tony Prieto chose one about the same size but it was white and orange glaze.

Another famous Japanese potter who taught a session at Mills was Hamada. Hamada's work was very standard. It was what our early work at Arts and Crafts was based on, what my work is really based on. I have a couple of Hamada plates.

The painter Diebenkorn was there at Arts and Crafts, and Oliveira. Hassel Smith and David Park were around. I met them at parties. Some of them went on to the Art Institute in San Francisco later, and then went off on teaching jobs, all over the place. I talked to the painters at Arts and Crafts, but we didn't get very buddy-buddy, although we passed each other often. We were awfully insulated, we were awfully self absorbed, the potters. And the painters were to themselves. We really didn't mix much at all. We were all so busy we didn't have much time to do much fooling around. And busy in a very happy kind of way. We went every lunch time, four or five of us, to eat in a little cafe around the corner. That was such fun!

All this time I kept hearing from my friend Margorie. When she was divorced by her husband in Alamagordo she was left without any reason to be there, because her breadwinner had departed. So she just rushed up to Santa Fe, where she had a friend or two, and began to go to the parties there, and she met a man named Rogaway, a painter. I had just met him here in Berkeley, at a party at the house of Lilik Shatz, another painter. Rogaway had been living here with the Shatzes, who were a Jewish family from Israel. The father was head of the university there in Tel Aviv. The mother and Lilik and his sister Zahara came to Berkeley on vacation, and the war came and they were stuck and couldn't get home for two years. They worked in the Richmond shipyards. When the war was over they all went back. I have a painting of Lilik's over my stairs. I had no sooner met Rogaway than he suddenly decided to go to New Mexico, I don't know why. A month after they met, Marge and Rog were married, there in Santa Fe. Then they went down to Mexico. Margorie had her first baby there—named Esther. Then in a while they went up to Taos.

Of course the first time we ever saw Taos was during the war, when we were in Alamagordo. But Margorie kept luring me back to Taos by talking about what was going on there, and the interesting things they were doing. And how beautiful it was. Finally one summer I went up there to help her find a piece of land. We found two acres on the stream near Ranchos de Taos. One was for Wallen and me. I lent her the money to buy her acre in exchange for paintings that Rogaway had done.

It was a Spanish woman who sold those two acres to us. Mostly the Spanish would not sell anything, but Margorie and Odelia were good friends. She was like one of the family. When Marge and Rog first went to Taos Odelia began to work for them. She was a lonely person, because she lived at the end of the valley, because she had a paralyzed mother, and because she was a Presbyterian, in this Catholic valley. So she didn't have any friends. She was very happy to have Marge and Rog as her friends. She sold us that land.

Wallen and I never did use our acre. But when Wallen came up later that summer we helped Marge and Rog build a little adobe house on their acre. We bought eight hundred dollars worth of adobe bricks, and we got several loads of pine poles, for Vegas, and we sat and planned the house with Marge and Rog.

We were living in the house of Mildred Crews, at the time. Margorie and Rog had rented a room from her. I rented a room from her, and my brother even came up for a while with his wife and rented one. Mildred had a fine house for parties, a long narrow house. She was living with her husband then. He was working on the newspaper. He was a poet. She was a photographer. I liked them. Mildred was always sad, you know, always terribly sad about something or other, and there were always plenty of things to be sad about—a lot of people with trouble. She knew them all. Mildred's husband was a sort of bushy type.

Rogaway was tall and had a sort of flat, inquisitive, curious face, with very beautiful soft brown eyes. He had a face that looked at you. But he didn't have very much hair, and he was always either dancing or singing or talking. He was an active person. He was a good dancer. He loved jazz and he would turn on the radio for jazz in the evenings when we were up there in Taos all together. He'd dance in a corner, just dance by himself. He was a smooth-looking man.

Margorie had made him some beautiful colored

shirts, and he wore plain slacks, but he always had a soft blue or a rose or gold shirt made out of some beautiful material like linen.

They were both urban people. He had been here at U.C. He had two very adventurous aunts in Oregon, and he spent quite a lot of time there. When he came down to U.C. he had a little jazz band in order to make a living. He also sold shoes. He had a very smooth way with people, you know, and he could fit them into beautiful expensive shoes.

That fall Wallen and I went home from Taos, and the next year I went up alone, because the next thing that happened was that I got a chance to buy a house on the highway. I bought this house from a young Spanish-American man for a thousand dollars, fifty dollars a month, out of my grocery money.

He felt it was being mistreated. It was four rooms in a line across a big lot, a hundred by two hundred feet. People lived in the house that this was attached to, and they were being careless and dirty about it. I'm not sure whether some of them lived in it, but they let the kids play all over it. It was kind of messy, not dirty really, but not cared for. So I bought it, and Wallen agreed to that, and then every year I would go out there ahead of him, in the summer, and stay with Marge and Rog and whitewash the walls of my house and oil the floors and all kinds of things.

We put in a water pipe, and a water well. We found a young man from Texas who was doing wells, and he came down and did it. That was another thousand dollars!

When Wallen came we gathered beautiful blue rocks from the Rio Grande and we made steps in front of our front door, because before you just stepped from the dirt onto the living room floor. Then I had a Spanish boy make a curved adobe wall from four feet away from the front door to the well house. He was *unable* to do a curved wall; he thought a wall should be straight and have corners. We wanted a curved wall because it looked nicer to have it run around the house that way. It gave us a little privacy from the highway, too; we were a hundred feet from the highway.

I did a little pottery in Taos, but I did it in the home of Frieda Lawrence. He was dead, of course, Lawrence. Marge and Rogaway had gotten to know everybody just by being there. He was an artist, and she was a gallery person. They met Frieda in the grocery store, I guess. I remember first *hearing* Frieda's voice in a grocery store, this enchanting, lovely thick voice of hers. It was like a song; you could hear it from across the room. A very deep, very rolling English-style voice, because she was educated in England. Gradually we got to know Frieda and her friend Brett, and they came and visited. Because I was a potter Margorie said, "You've got to find a place where you can work." So she tackled Frieda, who had this dashing Italian, Captain Ravagli, living with her. He had been a dear friend of Lawrence, and had come from Italy with him, and then he inherited Frieda and the ranch. He was a potter; he had a ceramic studio and a kiln and a wheel. So Margorie introduced me to Frieda, who was by then living in a big house north of Taos, not on the ranch. I used to go over and listen to her; she was very charming, with this beautiful voice, and loved to tell stories and hear stories. She was very sociable.

Then I'd go over to the studio and climb behind the wheel and do a little throwing. Ravagli would fire pots for me. Of course he was a very cock-of-the walk, a kind of a rooster of a man, and of course he chased every woman that he saw, including me. We all knew how to get out of his way. So it wasn't a very peaceful or restful place to be potting. Frieda knew about it, I suppose; everybody did. Everybody knew what he was like.

Frieda looked motherly. Like Margorie, only bigger. She was a Juno, a German Juno-type. But I wasn't terribly interested in either of them. I was glad that I could work there, I was glad I knew Frieda a little bit, but I didn't have a yearning to be deeply friendly with either of them. They were the social life of the village; now they were living near town, there where Brett was, about three miles north of Taos. They would entertain a lot. I did see the ranch before they moved away, and their house there, which was full of those paintings of Lawrence's, those bright pink nudes! Ravagli had built the chapel for Lawrence's body there.

Mabel Luhan wasn't there. I didn't know her. I never met Tony Luhan either, I never met either of them. I did know Dorothy Brett; I knew her quite well. She had a station wagon and a couple of dogs in the station wagon and she had an ear trumpet. You had to shout for Brett. She was small and very plump. She came to see Marge a lot, and then we all spent the afternoon; we had coffee and talked. Brett was a painter, and she did beautiful paintings of Indians. I wanted to buy one very much and I didn't ever do it. I could kick myself now because she did exquisite paintings of Indians.

In Taos you talked to everybody at gallery openings. Every Saturday night there was an opening. You just talked to everybody and everybody talked to you. There was a circular rim of small adobe houses around the edge of town. I made friends with a woman painter who had a lovely adobe house on this circle, west of town. Behind her was a big adobe wall and then there was a big adobe house which belonged to two artists. The wife was a New York woman, very dressy. I have a beautiful little painting of hers, white on white. All these painters were friends. There was a woman called Dorothy who sponsored the gallery near the Taos Inn. And of course they had evenings at the Taos Inn often; you met people and talked to people there.

Everybody broke up at the end of summer. Some went to Mexico for the winter, as a colony. Then next summer we'd all come back again, and be happy to see each other. We went to Taos for ten summers. In the fifties. You went to dinners, you went to visit people, you went on walks, you went to visit other smaller towns where there were beautiful pots and blankets for sale.

For me Taos was just full of interesting people. They were just sprouting out of everywhere. Everybody was so light-hearted and light-footed and coming and going, you know. Probably I couldn't find my old Taos any more. People would listen to each other's tales of woe by the hour, and be encouraging if possible. There was a lot of listening and helping. But you know, nobody seemed to take any of the misery too seriously; there was a certain drama in being miserable. We were broke, and so we invited each other for dinner, and it might be just a big stew.

I suppose people are less interested in each other than they used to be. The fine art of gossip! There was a lot to gossip about in Taos. People were swapping husbands and wives and all kinds of weird things.

You met a lot of people in Taos that you liked, and you saw quite breezily back and forth, easy going, but you didn't spend a lot of time with them, the way I spent time with Margorie. She meant a lot to me; I admired her, and I loved her a lot.

Then the trip to Taos began to seem too long. Thirteen hundred miles! We went all the different roads, until we knew them all, inch by inch. Then we decided to sell the house.

Nine

Cloverdale

Cherry didn't marry until after she graduated. She had studied physiotherapy in Sacramento, so she was a therapist, and she got a job in a clinic. In that clinic she met Wade, who was a friend of someone who worked there. They started this really exciting courtship, and Cherry couldn't make up her mind. Wade's mother said, "Please tell her to decide, because Wade is wasting away!" Anyway, she did decide, and then the plans for the wedding! It was to be in the little church on Dana and Bancroft, where Ben and Little Grannie always went Friday afternoon for the organ music. Cherry would drive them down and they would all sit in a row and listen to the music. They loved that little church, so we planned the wedding there. I got a notebook and

I planned it inch by inch, from the cake and the dresses to the guests and the packages and the invitation and everything. Then when I had all this set I went to New Mexico to visit Margorie. I didn't come back until the wedding, in June.

Ben and Little Grannie didn't go inside for the wedding. They didn't like the stale air. They stayed outside in the car—anyway, Ben didn't want to catch cold. They were just quirky. Cherry came out in her lovely wedding gown after the ceremony and talked to them.

Ben and Little Grannie were living in the Cottage. When that was first built it was just the one room with a little alcove that we called the coffee alcove. Everybody who lived in the Cottage—and we all lived in it from time to time—needed something added. The first thing was the kitchen, which had to be improved because it was half outdoors and it had a tree growing through it.

The next thing that happened was that we closed in this kind of pergola, a little long area that led to the garage and that Ben used for a little outside studio. We had that leveled off—I am absolutely insane about levels instead of stairs, so I planned it so that the kitchen floor and the pergola and the garage are all on the same level. We made a nice kitchen there, and the rest of the space became an outdoor living room, a porch, of railroad ties which we painted.

Ben did architectural drawings there, outside. He was retired by that time. He had a space, which is now the outside living room, and it was bowered by willow trees. He hung a sort of curtain all around and he had a couple of chairs and a drawing table. It was well protected, and he had it curtained against the wind.

The *main* addition came when Little Grannie got sick and Kerna added a bedroom, which we called the Green Room, for the nurse. She got caught by a City Inspector, who said, "Mrs. Maybeck!! I wouldn't think *you* would do this!" But they got it all straightened out.

And then when Sheila and Johnny came through from Okinawa on their tour of duty with their three children, after Ben died, something *really* had to be done. So we took the little bedroom and we excavated the hill from there and got a space that was twenty feet wide. Everybody, Sheila, Johnny, Wallen and I all dug into that hill and we had wheelbarrows and we made a terrace in front of the house with the dirt. The contractors poured a cement floor and they poured a wall, and they put an upstairs room on top. So all of a sudden we had two big bedrooms. The lower one was cement-block against that excavated hill, and the upstairs was wood.

In 1950 Wallen and I built the house next door, 2 Maybeck Twin Drive. Ben designed it, but not in his office—he was retired—at home. He just drew it out for us. We worked with him, Wallen and I, and said what we wanted and where we wanted it. We did some of the work. The family, Ben and Little Grannie, gave us the lot, and we decided where we thought the house ought to be, where we could get a view. We planned to live in it.

It was called Arilaga because we bought a second-hand door, a glass door for the front door. And on it in gold letters it said, "Arilaga Musical Academy." We loved it. We scraped off the "Academy" and the "Musical" and we left just "Arilaga." For a while people would come up and say, "Oh, I went to Arilaga Musical Academy," or "My son is going to the Arilaga Musical Academy." And then we had a tenant who scraped *that* off! We were so angry! Oh, well.

Ben and Wallen and I planned the house very carefully. The living room was not to be too big; we didn't have too much money. So Ben made the drawings and they bought the beams and set them in place and I went in and here was this rather small living room, not too high, with enormous beams across it. I knew I couldn't live in it, under those beams. And so I said, very diffidently, timidly, "I can't live in here. The beams have got to be smaller. They are bigger than the room." Consternation!! "We can't do that," the workmen said. "Mr. Maybeck

Ben and one of his drawings.

won't let us." I said, "Well, I have to live here, I'm paying for it, Wallen and I, and we can't go on with these beams." So eventually they took them down and they took them to the planing mill and cut off about two inches on one side. Ben was annoyed, but at the same time...He was a very gentle person and an understanding person, so he didn't stay annoyed. There were plenty of other things to worry about, and take care of.

The whole length of the room had a cement hob in front of the fireplace, with heating in it, water pipes with hot water in them, so that you could turn on the heat and sit on the warm hob by the fireplace. The bathroom floor is heated with water pipes too.

We poured the fireplace ourselves, weekend after weekend, two feet at a time. The floor is made out of navy hatch covers and we helped get those. The ceiling is sweetgum plywood from Hawaii. Red, Uncle Nick's son, was the contractor and builder; he had a crew working with him. We called them "The Dudes."

Later I did an awful lot of digging on the level place that the garage needed, and I had—of all people—Durvol Quitzow, the dancer, grandson of the Boyntons who built the Temple of the Wings, to help me. Durvol and I would dig and dig and dig and pull the dirt away and roll it down and level it. That dirt made my front lawn here at 2751.

We always thought we would live there, but then when it came right down to leaving this house... I had a Pot Shop here by that time, and Wallen had his basement workshop.

What a time we had with the Pot Shop, my studio behind 2751! There were a couple of eucalyptus trees there, and Wallen made a pulley from down where the garage is. We had a cement mixer and mixed the concrete down there. We had coal scuttles and a long chain and so I'd fill up a coal scuttle with mix and Wallen would heist it on up and pour it into the cement blocks. We built the whole room that way. It needed quite a lot of foundation, too. We built the walls with a lot of steel in them so it's well built. But it took a lot of cement!

Some time around then my parents died. They died before Ben and Little Grannie did. My mother died in 1950. We were up in Taos, and my aunt was with my mother. She wrote to me that my mother was sick and I came home from Taos. By that time my mother had grown worse. Wallen and Cherry went up and brought her down here to the hospital from the ranch. She died in about two or three days. She was in the house here, and getting worse, and then she was taken to the hospital and she died there. My father was here with us.

My father stayed with us a couple of days, and then we drove him back up to the ranch. He wanted to live there. He would have been welcome here, but he said no, the ranch was his home. His friends were up there, and he loved the ranch. He said he would be bored in town. So he stayed there. He lived there by himself for two more years. He died there.

A few years later Little Grannie died. She was in the hospital, and Ben just stayed there, beside the bed, all the time. They wanted him to leave, but you can't just throw a little old gentleman out! She just drifted away.

Ben died in the Cottage. He'd been living here with us. After Little Grannie died Kerna simply moved him in here with Wallen and me, without asking us. In a way it was hard on me and in a way it wasn't. It was kind of wonderful, because he was a very sweet man. And of course he wasn't as demanding of us as he was of Little Grannie. Sheila and little Adrienne were in the house with us; Johnny was away on duty in Iceland.

So there was a married couple, Wallen and me, there was Sheila—whose husband was away —with her little daughter, and there was Ben, an ancient gentleman, and there was Inez, the big black woman who took care of him, bathed him and dressed him, all in the house here. The baby was three years old. It was very smooth, but we were crowded, we were just crowded for space.

I thought that when he came here he would stay in the north room and spend a lot of time on the deck there, because it would be outdoors. No! The minute he heard a voice up here he came up the stairs and spent the day up here. He always wanted to be in on all the things that people were doing. He loved to sit at the table and have people come and have coffee with him.

You know that painting over the stairs, the one that Lilik Shatz did, with the Balinese bare-breasted women? Ben was always embarrassed by it. He thought it was rather horrifying that Wallen and I should hang naked ladies on our staircase! So he made a lot of brown paper clothes and pinned them on the ladies. I came home and I saw that...They said, kind of quiet, "Look what Ben did." I looked at it, and I was absolutely furious! I went right over and tore it all down. I said to Ben, "Don't you change Lilik's painting! Nodody would *dare* to change one of *your* paintings!" He didn't mean it as a joke. I don't think he had very much humor. He was whimsical and chuckly, but I don't think he had a great sense of humor at all. And he had a great thing about the sanctity of women, you know, the greatness of women...

It worked very well, having him here, really, except that it got very hard on me, in some ways, all these different interests, and different needs that had to be supplied. I was still teaching at Arts and Crafts. I went down there in daytime, on top of running the house and the family here. No wonder I got a little tired. Then every time I left the house Ben would say, "Where are you going?" I'd say, "I'm going down to the Safeway to buy a cabbage." Then he'd say, "When will you be back?" I felt oppressed; I wasn't free. Sometimes I didn't know when I would be back. If I was going down to Arts and Crafts I wouldn't know when I would be finished. But if I said to him, "I don't know," he would be hurt. He wanted me to be there.

I usually went in the summer to visit Margorie in Taos. But that year she and Rog were living in an apartment in Sag Harbor. So I took off and went to Sag Harbor for a month and experienced New England. We swam in the sound and we did all kinds of wonderful things. It was country. The country there was rather flat and flowing, and it was totally covered with small oak trees. There were a lot of artists there, interesting people. There was a little colony of well-to-do blacks from New York City. Nobody entered their domain, and you didn't go walking through their place. They had a piece of the beach and you felt very honored if you were invited to swim on their beach.

We knew a woman artist who had a little house in

the dunes and from her house she just walked over the top of the dunes and jumped into the Atlantic Ocean, which was kind of wild and very deep. I wouldn't swim; I was scared to death of it. But I was fascinated. She lived among all this sand; she had to sweep it off her porch all the time.

So it was very interesting, and at the end of the summer I'd rested up a bit, and I talked to Wallen on the phone—or wrote him; we wrote each other all the time—and I said I'd thought it all over and I wasn't coming home if Ben was going to be in the house any longer. After two years I'd got to the end of my endurance. And of course I always felt that Kerna should have taken him part of the time. She never did. She didn't get along with him so very well.

So Wallen and Sheila moved him out into the Cottage, with his nurse, because by this time he was really failing, and really infirm, and he was in bed a lot. I came home and two weeks later he died in the Cottage, with the nurse there to take care of him. She called up in the middle of the night and said he'd simply fallen out of bed, and he was dead.

Ben had designed the houses we built, Arilaga and Hilltop, but he didn't design Buckeye. He was gone by that time. About ten years after we did Arilaga we had enough money to do Buckeye. We finished that in 1960. It took a year to build. We

usually worked on our houses about a year, because
Wallen did an awful lot of work. He did all the elec-
trical wiring on both houses. I cut the railing up at
Buckeye myself out of redwood boards, with an elec-
tric jigsaw. We worked there on weekends, in the
sunshine. We had so much experience by that time
with Ben, and living in his kind of houses!

We had to subdivide the land to get permission to
build Buckeye. There had always been a driveway
up the side of the hill to the point, and we had called
it Via Tito, after Kerna's donkey, which was called
Tito. But during the war Tito wasn't a very popular
name, on account of the dictator of Yugoslavia who
was named Tito, and so we had to find another
name. We made the double driveway that is there
now, and we named it Maybeck Twin Drive, after
the twins, and because it was a double drive.

Again we leveled out the two levels and made the
driveway to the house site. We always wanted
houses that didn't have stairs, so we entered the lot
on a driveway, and went right into the garage and
the utility room and the kitchen and living room
all on one level.

I really designed the fireplace in Buckeye. It's a
triangular freestanding fireplace which is the
divider between the kitchen and the living room. I
like a fireplace on a hob; I like to sit by the fire and
put my feet up on a hob. I like it high; we did that up

at Buckeye. The fireplace is a foot above the floor, at least.

We didn't live there, but we went there and sat by the fire, sometimes. The Buckeye was our last house.

All the years that we went up to the ranch we always went through Cloverdale. So we got to know several people there, including Mrs. Foster and her son. The son, Arthur, was the owner of the National Bank in Cloverdale. Mrs. Foster was a lovely person of my mother's age, just delightful, and they had had a very large prune ranch, in Hopland. Arthur had this little bank, and then he bought a tract of land on the east side of Sulfur Creek, just out of town. It had an abandoned P.G.&E. building on it, an abandoned shell of concrete.

We always stopped at the Foster's place, and we went over the plans for making a house for Arthur out of this P.G.&E. building, which was enormous. He made a fifty by fifty foot living room, with a fireplace fifteen feet high, and then he had next to it a section that had two stories, with bedrooms on top, kitchen underneath, and below that, about twenty feet down, was the creek. You could swim in that creek. A marvelous place, and we often stopped there on our way to the ranch.

That's how we got to know Cloverdale. Then, when my mother and dad were gone, and we weren't going up to the ranch anymore, and we had sold the house in Taos, we bought land there. There were six little houses on the other side of the creek from Arthur's house, each on an acre. They belonged to Arthur. We wanted a place to take the grandchildren, who were growing up. Cherry and Wade were living in Santa Cruz, so they only came up to Cloverdale when they could, which wasn't very often. But Sheila and John were living in the Cottage, and they and the three children often went. We even went one weekend in the winter, when it snowed. We got caught in the snow on the road.

Our acre was flat, perfectly flat, with a tiny funny house which we spruced up as well as we could. It had an arbor in front of it, and it had a little barn, and it had this river. In the early part of the summer there were wonderful swimming holes. They gradually died off because they got full of algae, and bugs in the algae, and we didn't care much about that. But the kids loved it up there in Cloverdale. We'd all go up in the cars and open the car doors and everybody would fall out and start doing something they wanted to do.

One summer we all made paintings. We got canvas and pieces of wood and we made stretched canvases, ready to paint on, and we had paint and brushes. We hung all the paintings on the garage wall; it was a big blank wall that was near the kitchen. We all painted and we had a lot of fun with the kids. Not knowing anything about painting they did quite interesting things, naturally.

We built and rebuilt; we dragged rocks out of the creek and took them up and made little walls out of them where they were needed. We made paths. We painted the little barn red; we rebuilt the bathroom; we rebuilt the kitchen. We were busy all the time. Then we'd go to Arthur's to have a drink and dinner, walk across the creek up to our waists in water.

It was an interesting place. We only used it weekends. In about two years Wallen retired. Then he had four years before he died. He died on one of our rafting days—you could raft down the creek, *just*. He died very suddenly. We all went to bed and Wallen woke up and couldn't breathe. The girls and I got him into the car and rushed him to the little clinic in town, and called the doctor. Wallen died right there. He just never got his breath again. If you have to go, that's the way to go. But we were devastated.

When Wallen was gone there was no incentive for me to go to Cloverdale. Eventually I sold it, because you can't have a place you don't go to all the time and take care of it.

Ten

The Chimney Potters

In 1962, soon after Wallen died, Captain John Bathurst, Sheila's husband, was ordered out to Okinawa. Sheila and the children followed soon after. We went to Fairfax Army Transport and put them on a huge Air Force Transport plane. And there I was in Berkeley with no one I belonged to. I blindly put things in order and went to Okinawa too, in the spring of 1963.

I traveled in a one piece sleeveless white dress and black thongs. I couldn't have cared less. I spent a night near Honolulu—they put an orchid on my pillow! I had a room with screens but no glass. There were singers in the garden and sparrows on the breakfast table, eating crumbs.

I was met in Tokyo by an Air Force friend, and

was wafted to a stick-and-paper cottage in a cobbled compound. We went hunting for the Folk Museum that houses the work of Hamada, the great Japanese potter who had inspired us all at Arts and Crafts. We couldn't find a taxi driver who knew where it was. But we did find it, and we also found great stacks of Hamada plates for sale in a wonderful store in town.

To get to Okinawa I flew an hour in a small plane. There were little islands in the water, like pancakes. Okinawa was a pancake ten miles across and sixty miles wide. I found it wonderful! Hot! There were men in kimonos, going to the bathhouse at five o'clock in the evening. The black market had an alley. The smells...the beaches...and water like liquid jewels. There was a flower lady with a garbage can cover on her head full of flowers. There were sewing ladies who cut you a pattern and made you a dress for fifty cents an hour! There were potters, jewelry makers, and a factory to make flatware to sell to the United States. They were doing the delicate art of lacquer. Never do that on a windy day! Ten coats or more of lacquer on a wooden bowl or cup.

It was so hot I couldn't sleep. Sheila and John shut up the house and had fans going. I couldn't bear it and put on my grey kimono that made me invisible and I slept in a deck chair behind the house.

When a typhoon, grade one, was announced, we battened down everything and stayed inside. The typhoons boiled down from the China Sea, sometimes big, sometimes little. The native paper houses seemed to let the wind through.

We saw the caves where the inhabitants had hidden for two years after the United States Marines took the island. The Japanese military all threw themselves off the cliff. The hills near the towns were perforated with tunnels and caves full of munitions. We saw all this, and a lot more.

Of course I couldn't just stay there. I had a house to care for in Berkeley. I sadly tore myself away. I loved Okinawa; it was the most interesting place I ever visited.

I was still teaching at Arts and Crafts then. But I was getting older, and it wasn't so much fun any more. Everybody was gone. Of course I didn't know what I was doing, really, getting used to everything. Somebody said to me, "You shouldn't live alone."

Then Clela Collins said that she was in charge of foreign students, ones with scholarships, and she gave me a Japanese girl to live here with me. Yukako Okudira. I have a picture that she sent me just last week from New York. She's doing very well; she's an artist. She's a very modern artist. It was nice to hear from her after all this time.

I don't know what made her come to the United

States. She'd gone to an English school in Japan; her father had been a flyer, and I think he must have been killed. Anyway, this friend of mine, whose husband was a colonel in Japan, had gotten very interested in Japanese children who were orphans. So she sponsored Yukako, who wanted to come and study here. First Yukako went to a rich family in San Francisco, and they made her the bartender. She was having a very hard time, and so Clela withdrew her, took her away from there, and looked for someone else to give her to, and she picked me and said, "Now you take care of her." I remember going down to Clela's house on Arch Street and walking in and there was this great big Japanese girl, looking scared to pieces, and unable to talk. She could read English, all right, but she couldn't speak it.

But she got so she could. We used to sit at the breakfast table and I used to say, "Tea?" and then she'd learn that. And then I'd say, "Coffee," or I'd say, "Sugar?" She learned English; she picked it up fast. She was fun to have here.

She became very beautiful. She finished U.C. and she went to San Jose. She worked for a family there and went to Art School. She became a great photographer. She had a boyfriend, and lived with him. She asked her mother for permission. You always ask your parents, of course, if you may do this, and her mother said, "O.K.," and so she did.

She must have been here with me for the four years of college. I had no other tenants at that time, just Yuka. Having two at a time just happened. Friends...people who needed a room. It wasn't anything I sought after; they just happened.

After I got through teaching at Arts and Crafts I joined a group that called itself the Chimney Potters. They had been started in what had been a doll factory at the railroad track on Cedar Street. There were kilns there; these were dolls with china faces and hands and feet.

It was a great big place. So a group of us rented it so we could use the kilns. We called it the Chimneys because it had the chimneys of the kilns sticking up through the roof.

That group moved to near Leslie Ceramics, the ceramic supply store on San Pablo Avenue, run by the Japanese, Mr. Toki. His wife was one of our potters, Leslie Toki. She was one of the potters who came and studied at Arts and Crafts when we were all there. A very good potter. She had twin sons, and they were great big boys. When I was teaching I would go down there for supplies and Mr. Toki would come and say, "Professor Maybeck, how are you today?" Then one of his sons got my job, when I retired, so he became a professor, too, I guess.

We bought a lot of stuff there. They carried clay too, but we got most of our clay in truckloads from

Murphy's, in the Sierras. We did a lot of work and selling. We had our Chimney group sale about the fifth of December. We would send out invitations and have it in Ann Soule's back yard. Sometimes there would be two sales, sometimes even three.

I think I went to maybe two Art Festivals, because it's an awful job! I did take pots to the Art Festival in the Hall of Flowers in the Golden Gate Park once, because the Potters Association was having a great big sale, and we would each get a table. Bernadette Cole and I got a table together.

Usually we just made pots and had our sales. I usually made four or five hundred dollars. I never took pots to the stores. Bernadette did, and I did once. But it was so slow and poky, the selling…It was much better to do it at our sales, invite people. It would be a great big exciting thing, and we'd have a lot of fun. I was selling conventional things, bowls, and cups and saucers and plates. I did sell decorated plates, and I got better prices for those. I got twenty, thirty dollars a piece for them. That was quite a lot of money then. I still have some; I have a stack of them kind of hidden away in the Pot Shop.

One year, maybe it was last year, the B.A.H.A., the Berkeley Architectural Heritage Association, was having a Christmas party with a sale, and I gave them three of my beautiful old plates. They sold them for quite a good price.

Jacomena Maybeck in her Pot Shop.
(Photo Pamela Valois)

People and Places

I got involved with B.A.H.A. because they were going to have a Maybeck House Tour, and they asked me if they could place my house on the tour, would I let people through. This was probably in the seventies. This meant that I began to work with them, and talk with them, deciding the dates, and clearing the house to have it ready, and deciding what we would do about this and that and the other.

The house tours were to make money for our efforts for the whole year. We make about twenty thousand dollars on a house tour. Right now B.A.H.A. is giving money to a bunch of organizations who are suing the University for overgrowth, for demolishing whole historic buildings, and overbuilding. It's a general fund. Sometimes we lend somebody money, or help publish something. They published my little book about Maybeck. It cost around four thousand dollars. This year we're helping another author republish his book on Berkeley homes.

I'm not involved in the politics of B.A.H.A. particularly. I've been on the Board for about five or six years, maybe more, but it bores me. So much of their work is going down to City Hall and fighting for land grants, or getting landmark status for a house. Or fighting the demolition of something. I'm no good at these political committees, so what I've done, I've given them plates, I've given them my house to be on a house tour, I've sat in other houses on a tour—I've done things like that. Now I'm on the Board of Regents, emeritus.

My friends Margorie and Rogaway used to leave Taos to spend summers in Mexico. Wallen and I went to visit them there, several times, spent a month with them in Ajijic, near Guadalajara, or in San Miguel de Allende, where there is an art school, and a pottery school. Then they decided that they couldn't live in Mexico, for some reason, and they decided that they would go to Spain. They must have heard things that made them want to go there. They must have had a friend or two there, already, because they immediately went to a little tiny village called Mijas. It was seven miles above Fuingaroa, about fifty miles or so from Gibraltar, along the Mediterranean coast.

After Wallen died I went to visit Margorie there several summers. We would sit around in the sun, and then we would drop down from her house seven miles to the beach on the Mediterranean. They were wonderful beaches, and nobody was there yet.

One year I went from Spain to Naples with Margorie, because her sister was there. We were put on a little tender in Malaga and taken out to this big Italian steamer; they opened a hole in the side and they let down a little ladder and hoisted us up. We were on it three days. It was the most gorgeous food in the world, and Margorie, who was so plump, you know, loved deserts, and there were always three or four deserts and she had one of each! And then we'd take the cherries down to our stateroom.

When we got to Naples we went every night to see the sister, who was in the hospital. Finally, because they couldn't seem to cure her, the U.S. government from the base there sent an airplane and flew her to Germany. There were quantities of Spanish people in that hospital, especially children. We'd go and then we'd come home on the streetcar, in the evening, come back in the dark through the town of Naples; we'd walk down the street and the Italian boys would pinch us!

Marge and Rog spent the rest of their lives in Spain. They built an interesting house there. It was up and down a hill, made out of natural materials, with marble and slate for floors and tile walls, with beautiful views from each room. Margorie died in Spain, a couple of years ago. Then Rog came to where his daughter is living, in Tucson, Arizona. They drove out here one time a couple of years ago, and he was all dressed up in a beautiful tweed jacket. He was always very vain of his appearance. He loved beautiful clothes. I have a picture of him and Margorie on board a steamship, and they are just a very elegantly dressed tourist couple.

Rog is getting lots of money for his paintings now.

His daughter Esther is his agent, and she takes those paintings everywhere. She drives him to Los Angeles and Fresno, and they go to all the big stores, and leave the paintings. He is doing the same kind of painting, you know, distorted faces, only it's much better. Very gorgeous stuff now.

In 1978 I was retired from Arts and Crafts. I was spending a great deal of time at the Chimneys. Then the Chimneys disbanded. Ann Soule began to make sculpture instead of making pottery—she'd been a painter before. This drew an entirely different kind of buying public, those that wanted to spend a hundred and fifty dollars on some ducks or a pig or something. It changed the whole attitude of the sale. Mary Murchio especially got tired of the sale. I was selling fairly well, but not as well as I had been. Bernadette Cole wasn't selling well because people would come in order to buy these animals. She wanted to change her style, anyway, and she did. She got a store in Lafayette to sell her things and she had one up on the coast, in Gualala. She had various other places. She didn't mind doing that. I wouldn't do it. So we decided that the Chimneys just wasn't working. We just stopped. Another thing was that they raised the rent. First it went from twenty-five dollars a month to a hundred. We could pay this because we began by being ten of us down there. But then it got up to five hundred dollars and Mary and Bernadette and I dropped out because we didn't think we were getting enough back out. I haven't been part of that kind of group since.

After the Chimneys ended I went down to work at Berkeley High School, in the Adult School, with Ken Dierck in charge, and a fine kiln. I made new friends and good pots, but it was hard; the parking was so hard to find. Then Ken retired and the class closed. Then about five of us who had gotten to know each other there began to go up to Mary Murchios to work on her deck, in her wonderful garden. She began to fire some of our stuff. But that didn't work out well for me at all. For one thing you had to go down those long stairs, thirty-five steps. And...well, Bob Lu has a teapot of mine. He came a while ago and trimmed my persimmon tree and I gave him a teapot. He selected it, and he loves it, but it's as heavy as lead. The reason is that I would throw something one day at Mary's, and if I did that at home I could trim it the next day, cut the extra clay out of the bottom, but at Mary's I wouldn't be able to get back there to trim it for two or three days maybe, and then the darn thing would just dry up and I couldn't trim it any more. I appreciated what she did for us, letting us work there, and it was such a pleasant place to work, but it was ridiculous for me to try to be a potter under those circumstances.

And I don't really feel like using my own Pot Shop any more. I like working with people.

The next thing that happened was Branciforte. A few years ago I was feeling prosperous. My granddaughter Adrienne, Sheila's daughter, and her husband Dan McGuire were living in Santa Cruz; they were teachers and they had found jobs there. Dan's parents were happy to take them in, but it went on and on, and everybody was asking when Ade and Dan would find a house. How could they find a house, where could they live and have their own place...So finally I said, "If you can find a place you like I'll help you buy it. I'll put down the down payment."

They found a house on the way to town along that straight mile-long road of Branciforte. It was an old white Victorian house in the midst of about three acres of land, a big piece of land. It had five bedrooms and one bathroom, a kitchen, a living room, a washroom, a dining room and a music room. Five bedrooms!

Finally the old man who owned it decided he would sell it to us, and we bought it. Then we immediately divided the land into thirds and sold the rear third. That helped bring down the price. That left us with the other two-thirds, which was still a great big lot...well, for a town...

Ade and Dan moved in, and they took over the

payments. We began to modernize this old house. We found that everything was wrong with it. There was a little extra toilet in the back and it was running into the basement. We just took up the whole floor and put new stringers under it, and did a lot of digging of earth there, earth that had to come out. We put on a new roof, and in other words it is now a modern house, and we are very happy with it. It's a beautiful place. We've redone it inch by inch. And I've kept two big bedrooms, my bedroom and my own guest room, where I can go any time I want.

Eleven

After Retirement

Here I am free of a job. Retired. Well, now what? What is there in myself to work with, to enjoy with? Really, age is a damn nuisance. You have to work harder for everything. But magic things still happen!

I do have a job still; it is the care of the four houses that are my income and my home. Wallen and I built two of them; they are like children, always a problem, a leak in the roof, a sewer stopped up. We expected to live in each one we built, Arilaga in 1950, the Buckeye in 1960. Each time we just couldn't leave 2751. Wallen's basement full of tools, my Pot Shop, full of pots. But I keep my eye on those houses. I enjoy that. Sitting with a cup of coffee by the fire I think out problems and plan improvements. There is a special panel in my head for worry things. Let them stew a while and a solution pops up.

And there is what I call Grandmother Gardening. I have a foot problem and that has drastically cut my ability to garden on a steep hill. My house and garden are sixty-five years old. The basement level has a lower garden; the deer and I have compromised: they get the lower garden to sleep in, to eat everything, maybe to have babies in the bushes. The second level garden has a screen over the flower bed. Flowers don't really thrive but the deer are thwarted. They mostly come by at dusk or dawn and sniff the plants. The third garden starts at the third floor, the kitchen door. It has a little brick patio, a couch, and a row of potted plants. Then it rises in one-foot terraces and steps, up the hill: four steps and a path, more steps and a higher path. That one is the deer's road from neighbor garden to neighbor garden. Since I've become a Grandmother Gardener I've given that one up. But I fiercely defend terraces one and two.

A Grandmother Garden should have a couch and a comfortable chair to view the garden from. She can study the "Magic Garden" booklets and learn about deer-proof plants.

This October the glorious pink amaryllis are still in bloom. Also shasta daisies. I plant lavenders, salvias, sedams, which the deer eschew, while they chew on roses and petunias. Zinnias are a godsend.

A grandmother can weed and plant any flower bed as wide as her arm is long. Long-handled pointed hoes are great! Toy rakes! The very *best* pruning shears, several kinds, and keep them sharp! A weeding tool.

I bragged about my one-flower garden. The one flower was a pink dahlia. It was eaten once and came again, and I laid a chicken wire entanglement around it and it bloomed for three weeks.

Of course deer are beautiful, too. They catch your breath as they trip through your garden. So these years it's house and dinners and garden. If Maybeck had known I would live so long he would have built us a house without stairs and not on this steep lot. But he did and we had it and I love it.

People become so important as the years go on. Each one is a story, a drama, a challenge to understand and to enjoy. And of course the people nearest and dearest are always the family. Our little bunch, Wallen and I and the twins. The twins...I haven't talked about them very much; there is too much to say. They shone like little stars in our lives. And their children! Again an enchantment of names: Adriana and Sheila Kern, our twins...their school lives and marriages out of which blossomed their children, Mark, Scott, Sheila K., Adrienne, Kerrie,

John Xavier. Now in 1991 a whole school of new babies, Cean, Scott-Hamilton and Peter; Steven and Bryan; Breanna and Allison. Even a crowning glory of twins! Keegan and Catherine Jacomena! I've been down to see them, and I try to help. So much work just to feed those voracious mites! Eat and sleep, cry a bit, be rocked. What a life! While the parents wonder what hit them!